STORIES FROM A SMALL TOWN

Enjoy the stories.

Best

Roger

STORIES

{FROM A SMALL TOWN}

Remembering My Childhood
in Hedgesville, West Virginia

ROGER ENGLE

GIRLS ON PRESS
MARTINSBURG, WV

GIRLS ON PRESS
the publishing imprint of STEPHANIE ENGLE DESIGN OFFICE

Post Office Box 6154
Martinsburg, WV 25402

WWW.GIRLSONPRESS.COM

FIRST EDITION PUBLISHED 2012. SECOND PRINTING 2013.
Printed in the United States of America

18 17 16 15 14 13   2 3 4 5
ISBN: 978-0-9857134-0-9

LIBRARY OF CONGRESS CONTROL NUMBER: 2012940913

This book is printed on acid-free paper.

CONTENTS

PREFACE

ALMOST A DECADE AGO SOMETHING TRIGGERED a memory from my childhood. A few more memories followed, so I decided to write them down. I added more over the next year, and they grew into a rather long list. Each entry was only a word or two — just enough to keep each thought alive.

On a cold winter day, I decided to take one of those thoughts and write a little more about it — it would be a good thing to give to my children. As I began writing, I realized it was possibly more of a selfish thing I was doing, for it opened the door to memories I had almost forgotten. It felt good to recount these stories and events and conjure up images from a time long gone.

As I continued the process I realized how precious and fleeting memories are. We assume that we'll always be able to get that information, but sometimes that's not possible. It's too late to ask my parents about their childhoods. I have only the few bits and pieces they volunteered.

My children are busy with their lives and may have little interest in my childhood now, but they may later. In the event I am unable to tell them later, or am long gone, I have attempted to create a snapshot of my childhood.

The following stories are not so developed as to be a novel, but rather serve as glimpses of what I remember as real life while growing up. I would encourage everyone to write down their stories to pass on, as each person's life is unique. I believe everyone has at least one book in them, and this is a start at writing mine. You should begin yours.

INTRODUCTION

IN 1972, I WATCHED *THE HOMECOMING* ON TV for the first time. Based on the book written by Earl Hamner, Jr., the movie is about a family living on Walton's Mountain and the challenges they face living in the 1930s and 1940s.

From *The Homecoming* movie came the *Walton's* TV series, which aired for nine years. I identified with this storyline in a personal way, even though 20 years separated the times depicted on Walton's Mountain from the time of my upbringing in Hedgesville, West Virginia. I found that many of Hamner's experiences paralleled my own. Although he had more siblings than I did, we both had grandparents living in our home and a close extended family located within a small area. My neighbors were much like his, along with a town store serving as a focal point.

Later on I got a copy of the book and learned that he took the characters and setting from his surroundings, but the story line was mostly fiction. My wife and I went to visit his hometown of Schuyler, Virginia. The town that served as the basis for the fictional setting of Walton's Mountain houses a museum showcasing scenes from the TV show. The Hamner home still remains.

In a snapshot, the town is nothing like the Walton's setting in the show. This was not a disappointment, just a fact. I feel sure many of the shows had at their core a glimpse of Mr. Hamner's childhood experiences.

Schuyler, Virginia, was as isolated and self-contained to Earl Hamner as Hedgesville was to me. Both towns had one major employer. Community life was centered around church and school. The town store provided just about everything you needed, and the Sears catalog did the rest. Family and friends kept a watchful eye on everything.

A feeling of self-sufficiency prevailed. To a child, your world is as big as the distance you are able to explore. You are not isolated, but rather protected by this fact. Both Schuyler and Hedgesville, I believe, offered the protected environment in which one's childhood experiences could leave cherished memories.

Only 10 miles away from Hedgesville was Martinsburg, but to a child it could have been 100. It was a larger town with stores, banks, offices, and restaurants. There were hospitals, theaters, fire and police departments. It had all the trappings of a bigger town. These things didn't exist in Hedgesville. Friends who grew up in Martinsburg have a completely different setting for their childhood. No better or worse, just different. I can't imagine what it was like for them.

I feel my childhood experiences marked the end of that feeling of isolation within the community and certainly the end of the freedom to roam the countryside as a child. It was the end of community security under the watchful eyes of family and neighbors. Perhaps it was the end of trust.

No generation can recreate its exact conditions for the next. You just can't. Children today don't understand the self-sufficient community idea. As a child, a mile was a long distance to travel. Not so today. Travel today is a part of life. Parents take their children 25 to 50 miles away for shopping, eating, or sporting events. What can't be attended in person can be joined on the Internet.

This book documents my memories of growing up in a very small town between the years of 1948 and 1964. The geographical location, along with the community, my family, friends, and acquaintances created a very unique environment in which to be a child. Although the stories of Walton's Mountain had many similarities to the stories of my upbringing in Hedgesville, they differ in one significant way: my stories contain no fiction. They are composed of the real people, places, and events that made up my world. This was my childhood.

PART ONE

A PLACE CALLED HOME

The Beginning

EVERYONE IS BORN AND GROWS UP SOMEWHERE during a certain period of time. We don't get to choose any of the variables. They help make us who we are. We don't think about them as young children, but drift back to them as we get older. Some memories are good and others are not. We have a way of putting a different spin on them and alter them to make us feel good.

My stories cover the years between 1948 and 1964. We are familiar with stories written about pioneers, economic depression, and wars and how they impacted someone living in a specific region. The Hollywood versions of these times are designed to entertain us.

I was born in April 1948, and spent the first 21 years of my life in Hedgesville, a small community in the Eastern Panhandle of West Virginia, situated in a gap along North Mountain on State Route 9. Histories have been written describing the area and events that occurred there and in the vicinity. None of this is important when you are young.

As towns go, it had almost nothing and yet everything a child could need. It existed before the days of interstate highways and shopping malls. We had a very small post office, a barber shop, a greasy spoon restaurant, a garage, several churches, a town spring, and a general store. There was a small elementary school and a combined junior and senior high school. A pool hall lasted a few years. In later years a volunteer fire department was established. That was it for my town. There had been a dentist, a doctor, another store, an undertaker, and even a hotel, but all were short-lived and most just memories shared by adults.

Hedgesville was really nothing but a collection of houses built near the intersection of two roads, with a couple of streets and alleys. There were about 100 homes and perhaps as many as 400 residents. I'm not sure of the exact number because people living nearby, but outside the town limits, still considered themselves to be residents.

As a child, I never counted or cared. The town was home to working-class families with children of all ages. There were about a dozen kids my age, but since we all had different ideas of "fun," we were rarely all together at the same time. Hedgesville had a fair share of elderly people — especially older ladies who neither married nor had kids. We referred to them as "Old Maids."

There were no factories or places of employment in the town; the closest source of work beyond the local farms and orchards was a brick manufacturing plant. The county seat of Martinsburg was 10 miles away and offered jobs at the hospital, various factories, and shops. My father worked at the brick plant and my mother was a homemaker for many years. Later in her life she worked as a nurse's aide in Martinsburg, and then as a teacher's aide in Hedgesville.

Our first house was a rental located beside the old post office and close to the town spring. It had no running water and a two-burner kerosene stove for cooking and warmth. At this age I have very few memories, but I do remember playing in a large puddle of water that collected between us and the adjoining house. I also remember a neighbor who kept stealing our kerosene. It was while living here that I got very sick and had to have my appendix removed.

Our second house was larger and equally ill equipped with modern conveniences, with the exception of a pitcher pump in the kitchen. However, the house was located next to the Brown's, who had milk cows and provided us with fresh milk in bottles with the cream on top.

I don't want to get ahead of myself, but I must say something about my grandparents on my father's side. They lived in Charles Town, West Virginia, and my grandfather was an auctioneer who died the same year I was born. My grandmother, "Nanny," didn't drive. We sometimes drove the 25 miles to her house or picked her up at the bus stop in Martinsburg. I remember walking with her before we moved into our second house. We stopped at what would become our new home, and we sat on the smokehouse steps. She asked me if I would like to live in the adjoining house. Shortly after we moved in, she died. I was six. My father was an only child, and his parents' home in Charles Town was full of furniture. Receiving all of it forced us to look for a bigger house. We purchased our third house, the Beall house, in 1954, and did some repairs to it during the fall while being hit by Hurricane Hazel. We moved in that November. My mother lived there until her death. For my brother, sister, and me, it was "home."

The house was one of the first built in the town in 1830. It was large and had five bedrooms, along with a coal furnace and indoor plumbing. In spite of this, one of the first things we did was to dig a hole and construct an outhouse. It wasn't the last time we did this. The house had no heat upstairs — none at all. Have you ever placed your feet on a cold linoleum floor? We had a small barn and a chicken coop. Most houses in town had either a well or a cistern, and an outhouse. Some homes had hog pens. We kept our hogs with my mother's parents or a friend, but raised many chickens in our own backyard.

I feel very fortunate to have grown up in this setting. The 1950s for us were nothing like what you see on TV. I had the best of both worlds. My parents knew the Great Depression, and we lived with values formed during that time. The world was changing around us but we didn't see much of it. It was good. I find myself using the expression, "I feel like the last dinosaur." As I look back it was like a mild form of isolation. That is probably what made it so good. Money was rarely of concern to us kids because there were so many things to do that didn't cost a penny.

A town so small meant that you knew almost every resident, and you were related to a large number of them.

At that time, small towns were largely populated by just a few families who never moved away. Hedgesville was no exception. My two uncles, along with their wives and children — and a much larger extended family — lived there. My mother's family had lived there for several generations. Her grandfather was the town blacksmith and owned the first gas pump. He was also a woodcarver. My grandmother and her sister had married brothers from the McCarty family, so the list of relatives grew. Grandfather McCarty died in 1956. My Grandmother McCarty moved in with us — yet another adult to answer to. Those who were not related might as well have been. We had no locked doors and received much advice from all adults.

In this small town, options seemed endless to a boy my age. From the center of town it was less than five minutes to a variety of activities: hunting squirrels, turkey, or deer behind our house or rabbits and muskrat near the elementary school; fishing at either Pitzer's or Brown's pond and collecting frogs and salamanders from the town spring; playing ball games in yards, gardens, church lots, or at the schools.

Loafing on the corner usually led to some group activity. Some kids were totally sports-oriented and played games from daylight to dark. I found myself able to drift in and out of those games. Fishing and hunting could be done alone or in groups, each with different rewards. You could change activities at will, several times a day. This was the beauty of my location and available playmates.

The last part of the equation is my siblings. I have a brother four years younger than I and a sister eight years younger. That is just enough of an age difference to make many of our ideas of fun completely different, although my brother and I both found the woods and streams to be the best. He never gave up hunting and still does it today.

A picture is still worth a thousand words. If you go to Hedgesville today, the same intersection of roads exists, along with the addition of a stoplight. The store is gone, along with the restaurant and pool hall; the post office moved out of town; and some homes have been torn down. In spite of this, the overall character of the setting is still there and you can get a feel for the place. It's not the same, but I can fill in the missing pieces in my mind.

My hope is to keep alive in my memory the stories of my childhood, and also to share them with you. I lived in a time of transition, having the best of the past and the promise of the future. We were somewhat isolated, but it was probably by choice. I lived in my grandparents' and parents' worlds as well as my own. We made do. Old ideas die hard. Picking beans, feeding chickens, swimming in the creek, and watching Sputnik all happened together. The world was changing around us, but we seemed to hang on to the past and slowly embrace the future.

There is no order to the following stories. I tell them to you as best as I can remember and as accurately as possible. I hope you can visualize some parts and perhaps relate them to your own childhood experiences. We all had them — not necessarily better or worse than anyone else's — but certainly very different.

NICKNAMES

MANY PEOPLE IN HEDGESVILLE WERE GIVEN nicknames. The reasons why are as varied as the names themselves. I never got one and don't know why, but did just fine without. There were some residents who received several. If you assigned a nickname to someone based on a physical attribute, I wonder how they took it. If the name was given for some fearless or ridiculous act, it may have been a badge of courage.

My brother did receive a nickname or perhaps gave it to himself. It was *Deedle*. I have no idea where it came from but I always remember hearing it. I still use it today. His name is David, so you figure it out. This type of nickname has no connection to any of the above mentioned criteria for attachment.

Here are some of the nicknames we heard around town: *Bear, Beef, Bird Legs, Boo, Boodlers, Canhole, Deacon, Doc, Dooper, Flea, Fluff, Hams, Hoggy, Horse, Hound Dog, Miser, Nip, Peck, Pee Wee, Pig Nose, Pooney, Punch, Ribby, Scruff, Snooks, Sox, Spivis, Suicide, Tank, Thart, Tyke, Weasel, Weetzer,* and *Whitey.*

Some families just oozed nicknames, with members having several. It's amazing how a name sticks. The question is whether or not to use them today when meeting these people. You never asked how they felt about them as kids and certainly wouldn't bring it up some 50 years later.

The Great Bashing of Deedle

SOME PEOPLE ARE HARDHEADED AND SOME HAVE hard heads. My brother's forehead had an unusual attraction for hard objects. During a softball game in our yard, my brother was playing catcher. I don't recall who was at bat, but after the ball was hit, the bat was thrown. It hit Deedle directly on the forehead, over his nose. It made a good gash. This was the kind of cut that heals very slowly after forming a hard, dark, raised scab.

Some time goes by and we find ourselves playing a game of Hide-and-Seek. Our backyard offered some good hiding places. There were large pine and maple trees. The maples had limbs with enough diameter to allow you to lie on top of them, looking like a Cheshire cat.

Deedle decided to use none of these places, but rather to go across the alley to where the Methodist Church was constructing an educational building. He climbed some scaffolding and hid behind the concrete blocks that were stacked there. Unfortunately, he fell from the scaffolding, hit his head on some of the blocks, and reopened the cut. He bled like a stuck pig. I carried him home.

After a while there was another ball game. Hoggy was at bat and everyone knew he had a tendency to throw the bat. To avoid another accident, Deedle decided to hide in the bushes. After hitting the ball, as anticipated, Hoggy let the bat fly. But guess what? It went directly into the bushes and hit Deedle right in the forehead. This began a period of sideline observing with little participation. I can still picture him with his ugly scab of honor and a huge goose egg. They stood out clearly on someone with fair skin and light hair.

⸻

THE SCALPING OF BETH

MY SISTER BETH WAS BORN WHEN I WAS EIGHT years old. The announcement was made to me by a cook in the school cafeteria as I went through the line. The cook was also our neighbor. Deedle was four at this time. At two years of age, Beth had a pretty good head of curly brown hair. My mother took great pride in it, combing it often and adorning it with bows. These were things she didn't try on my brother or me.

Our living room was large and all the furniture was placed against a wall except on rare occasions. Sometimes the couch would be placed diagonally in a corner. This created a small triangular play area for us. Add a blanket over the top, clip on some clothespins, and you had a roof.

My brother and sister were playing in this area and things were unusually quiet — until I heard my mother yell. Then I looked at my sister and saw that many of her curls were gone. After some questioning, it was determined that Deedle had cut them off with Mom's pinking shears and hid the locks under the sofa. He probably saved me by doing it first.

Lest we ever forget this event, the hair was enshrined in plastic and placed in a desk drawer. A picture of my sister before the "scalping" was hung by the TV. I don't know if its placement was intentional, but you couldn't help but see it from all parts of the room.

Piano Lessons and Guitars

I DON'T BELIEVE I WAS EVER SMALL. I SEEMED TO BE taller than most other kids my age at a time when I wanted nothing more than to fit in and be a part of the gang. The idea of taking piano lessons was absolutely foreign to the kids I played with.

Music had always interested me. In the parlor was a piano that we inherited from my father's family in Charles Town. Playing by ear was easy for me. If I heard it, I could usually play it. My parents thought it would be good for me to take piano lessons. They were given by the Methodist Church organist at her home, up near the high school.

The fact that you were taking piano lessons was not something you shared with your friends. In order to take them, I had to walk to my teacher's house which was about half a mile away. Getting there required walking through town, trying to conceal my book. This was difficult because it was a rather large red and white book titled *Teaching Little Fingers to Play*, by John Thompson. I began this story by saying I was tall. Due to this, I was not a stealth piano-lesson-taker. It wasn't long before I was discovered and confronted as to where I was going. There was only one reason for me to be going to the teacher's home.

This was the 1950s and rock and roll was just catching on. Music was not a subject that came up in kid discussions at the time like it does today. Kids in Hedgesville received their music education from a traveling teacher and a flute-like instrument called a tonette.

Back to the lessons. I don't recall how long they lasted —

perhaps a few months at the most — but I do recall how they ended. I was sitting at the piano with my teacher when she excused herself to go to the kitchen, leaving me with instructions regarding which classical drills I was to keep practicing. Shortly after she left, I began playing C, F, and G chords with a rock-and-roll beat. She returned to the room and told me that my lessons were over forever. I really don't believe she thought I had learned everything there was to know about playing piano. I was certain, however, that she knew nothing about playing rock-and-roll music.

It was about this time that I got my first guitar. It was black and white and made totally of plastic, including the strings. I had absolutely no instructions and didn't even know how to tune it. I would sit in a swing under the cherry tree, adjusting the strings until I got a chord-like sound. Moving up and down the neck, I could produce different chords.

Upon studying a book about both notes and chord positions, I was able to figure out how to tune the guitar. I played the heck out of it. It became the thing I did a lot of the time. After a while I got a better one made of wood. My father later said that I might get an electric guitar for Christmas that year.

Our search for the electric guitar began in Hagerstown, Maryland, and included my first trip to a pawn shop. Nothing was found that was affordable. Sometime later while in Winchester, Virginia, we went to a Montgomery Ward store, and there it was. Still black and white and made of wood, but complete with a small amplifier. Somehow, louder is always better.

Playing chords and fingering came easy to me. My father noticed this and apparently bragged about my ability to some people at the brick plant, including his friend Woody. I was driven to his home and introduced to "country music." Country music in the 1950s was three or four chords. I learned some songs from Woody but never played with him publicly until years later.

I then joined the first group of musicians with whom I would make a public appearance. Being about 13 years old at the time, I was driven to and from the home of two of the musicians for practice. This was an experience in itself as they lived up a hollow. Reaching their home required fording a stream. A kerosene stove, curtains draped in the doorways, and stale air lingering under a bare light bulb hanging from the ceiling made up our practice location.

After some practice sessions, we were off to play. My first engagement with them was at a church. Four of us made up the group, but the congregation didn't hear a quartet that day. Before our set began, I noticed one of the musicians sweating quite a bit and I thought it was stage fright. Soon I realized it wasn't nerves at all, but alcohol consumption. We thus became a trio, played a few songs, and left.

Our town had a fledgling fire department composed of a 1941 Mack pumper, and they held a festival each summer to raise money to operate it. A few of the festivals were held directly behind the fire hall in Pitzer's field, but soon were moved to the elementary school. This was one of the social highlights of the town.

I played at this festival with *The Berkeley Travelers* several times. A flatbed trailer served as the stage. This was the kind of trailer with metal bands running its entire length. If the trailer was wet and you touched a microphone, especially with your mouth, you would receive a terrible shock and feel the buzzing in your mouth for some time. Some of the crowd listened to our versions of old country favorites. We were decked out in our finest country duds and played the best we could. No one complained as the concert was free to the public, and we were unpaid.

We even went so far as to enter a music competition at the Apple Blossom Festival in Winchester. I can remember sitting in that large armory building, waiting our turn. We were called to the stage and plugged into their amplifiers. This probably doesn't seem important, but it was amazing to share such expensive equipment with bands such as Bill Peer's *The Melody Boys*. Patsy Cline had even sang with this group. I should recall this better, but I must have been really scared or having an out-of-body experience. We played our songs, and I believe some of his band members joined in, but I'm not sure. For a young boy from Hedgesville, this was the big time — a stage filled with professional equipment, and lots of cowboys and girls!

Not long after this I was introduced to Patsy Cline, who was sitting in our living room with her children. She had been brought there by my mother's cousin who lived near her and was a close friend. I remember thinking that a big star was to be glamorous; she wasn't. A star was to talk nice; she didn't. In fact, I vividly remember her sitting in a rocking chair beside my grandmother with one of her children, saying that her kids would just *shit* anywhere. This was a word I couldn't use. My grandmother certainly would not say this, and she just kept rocking. Patsy visited a few times, and this probably would have meant more to me except that rock and roll was catching on and I was hooked.

Our first house in Hedgesville had an outhouse. I recently spoke to the owner and he told me that it is still standing. He said he keeps it because it was once used by Patsy Cline. Evidently, I shared more with Patsy Cline than I realized.

I left the country group, but returned for an occasional session or dance when they needed someone to fill in. I then decided to start a rock-and-roll band. It began in my parents' parlor with Scott Small on piano, Ralph Clem on drums, and me on guitar. What a racket among all of the antique furniture! When Ralph left the band, Scott took over on the drums. Members came and went, and at one time or another included Tom Cummings, Dave Barnhart, and Walt Duke. Others joined in later years from outside the area. Scott and I were the core and stayed together all through high school and even into our first year of college.

We practiced often at his home and mine. Our first performance was at the high school as part of a music program. We played the town festival as a group called *The Marauders* and did many dances and parties. I don't know how good we really were. We certainly were unique for the community as we were the only rock group at the school.

There is an unusual twist to this whole band experience that I must mention. Bill Peer was a well-known musician in the area, and Patsy Cline sang with his band. Bill Peer had a son named Larry, who played in a rock-and-roll band called *The Rejects*. They were managed by Larry Palmer, who also managed a car lot. I didn't know of his connection to this band when I bought a 1954 Ford from him — which, incidentally, I blew up in only one day. I also didn't know he had a younger sister named Gula. I later began dating her and ended up playing with *The Rejects*. On our first date I brought my guitar. What a long distance to travel in just a few years. What began as piano lessons brought me to my future wife. Gula and I were married in 1969.

Most kids in town had no interest in music in the 1950s. It didn't completely dominate my life, but it was a big part. I wonder what could have happened if my piano lessons hadn't ended, or if Patsy Cline had not died. Perhaps she might have helped me get into the music business. Music provided the vehicle that allowed me to see beyond the town limits and left me with memories of many good times.

BUTCHERING

HOGS WERE A PRIZED SOURCE OF MEAT, AND AS A kid, I was only to touch the fringe of the butchering process. My grandfather had a pen where we kept our hogs, and my cousins and I got to feed or slop them. A disgusting mixture of feed and water was poured or scraped from a bucket down a wooden shoot into the trough. The pigs would grunt, fight, and shove each other around in the process of eating. The pen smelled awful, and pig waste is about as bad as it gets.

We owned property that had a pigpen on it. The lot was on a steep hill and we used it only a short while, selling it to the Nadenbousch family who built a house there. Some pigs were kept down the alley at the Pitzer's house.

Butchering was a multi-day event. The equipment was set up at one site — either at Wasson's or our garden — and the animals were brought to a central area to process. You began several days before by digging pits for the scalding tank and lard kettles. Boards were laid out to form tables and wood was collected for fires.

Fires were started way before sunrise. The hogs were killed in their pens and loaded onto a truck and hauled to the butchering site. This event happened in November, usually during the week of Thanksgiving. Skilled men who had done this all their lives performed the complicated tasks. As the day progressed, some became less skilled due to the alcohol they consumed; there was a lot more conversation and less work being done, but the operation always got completed.

We kids tended the fires and stirred the lard kettles. The women moved between the kitchen and the butchering area, bringing in supplies and taking away freshly wrapped meat to be frozen. Hams were taken to the smokehouse where sugar and spices were injected and rubbed onto them for curing. We never smoked the hams. Country ham was the "primo" reward. We would sneak into the smokehouse in the following weeks and cut pieces of the ham away, eating them raw. Spices were packed back into the cuts to avoid detection. I'm surprised we never got sick.

Everyone ate well during butchering — the women saw to this. The process involved a dozen or so men, women, and children and an entire day to butcher several hogs. There were always the watchers who would stop by and offer advice even if you didn't want it. Some stopped by looking for handouts or specific pig items, such as brains.

The brains were mixed with eggs and eaten. I never got up enough courage to try this "delicacy."

When the day was over, everyone went home well after dark. Some helpers took meat as their payment, but as this was a family affair, your payment was to help with the next batch of hogs — usually the next day at the same location. Sometimes there were enough hogs to make the process last several days. If the timing didn't work out, the equipment was packed up and moved to a relative's house for later use.

I haven't seen a butchering in many years. Most people today have never seen a hog rolled into a scalding tank and pulled out steaming to be scraped clean. I can't imagine what they'd think if they saw a hog strung up above the ground on a tripod, be slit open, and have its insides spill out into big metal tubs and overflow onto the ground. Less sausage would be eaten for sure if everyone had to clean the pig intestine in order to fill it with sausage meat.

Butchering was a practical, necessary, and social event. It kept the family together, and you didn't have to be asked to help. There was a job for everyone and you were expected to do it well. Butchering was just part of our life and it had many rewards.

—∞∞∞—

LARD

ONE HUNDRED PERCENT PURE WHITE PIG FAT with no additives or coloring — that's lard. It is derived from boiling chunks of fatty pig tissue in an iron kettle over an open fire. It was necessary to stir often, and this job was done by us kids. It was hard to make a mistake. After many hours of boiling, the fat was squeezed through a press and the lard was poured into five-gallon metal cans to cool and harden.

Our supply was replenished each November following butchering. We placed the cans on our enclosed side porch and kept one in the pantry. No vegetable oil, no olive oil, no canola oil, and no shortening. We had lard. The more you used it, the messier it got. It was on the outside of the can as well as the lid. The emptier the can became, the greater the chance of greasing your arms as you dug deeper. Eventually the can got so messy you could hardly remove the lid. There was no chance of the lid or can rusting as air never came in contact with it.

Almost everything we ate was cooked in lard. An iron skillet was placed on the stove, a long spoon was dipped into the can of lard, and a blob was tossed into the skillet.

When heated, it looked like any of the healthy products we use today, but it wasn't. It was lard.

The food to be cooked was placed into this clear hot liquid. Most people today think that frying such things as potatoes or chicken requires a small amount of oil. We had our food submerged in several inches of bubbling pig fat. We had our own homemade bacon and hamburger. It wasn't 90 percent lean or *any* percent lean. If cooked alone, this meat could generate enough grease to fill a soup bowl. Combined with the lard, our hamburgers would float and the skillet could almost overflow with fat. You had to remove the hamburgers from the skillet, place them on a tilted plate, and then press them to remove some of the fat or else they would soak the bun. Potatoes, on the other hand, would absorb the liquid and hold volumes of lard. They smelled so good.

When my wife and I shop today, we study the product labels for nutritional values and tend to buy nonfat or reduced-fat products. We season them up to make them taste better. We had never heard of cholesterol or saturated fat as children. I wonder how high a cholesterol reading we would have gotten? I believe that we would've topped the charts — we had lard.

—◦◦◦—

CHICKENS

W E WERE NEVER WITHOUT CHICKENS. OUR chicken house was built near the barn and consisted of rough-cut lumber covered with tar paper. It even had a tar-paper roof. There was a window and door in the front, and a small door for the birds to leave the building and enter a fenced yard.

In early March we would drive to Martinsburg and return with several hundred peeps that we had ordered from the hatchery, which is just two blocks down the street from where my wife and I now live. In our chicken house, two large hoods containing heat lamps hung just several inches above the floor. This was the only heat source for the building. Mason jars screwed onto watering bases, and long trays filled with feed were added.

Peeps liked to bunch up under the hoods, so we checked them often and rearranged them as necessary. Although some peeps died, enough survived to make the venture worthwhile. Some peeps would have waste stuck to their tail feathers forming rather disgusting-looking masses. We caught these peeps, brought them into the house, and blotted them clean with warm water. It was not pleasant.

They grew rapidly and, as the weather allowed, ventured out into the fenced yard. It was around Easter time when a store in Martinsburg would display chickens and ducks in their window. These birds had been dyed pastel colors. For some reason we usually bought a few. When released into our flock they stood out like a sore thumb. They retained the color for their entire lives, and when it came time for them to leave this world, they received special treatment.

Towards mid-summer some hens began to lay eggs. The shells of the first eggs were not hard — just a membrane — but the contents were still edible. When egg-laying began, the type of feed given to the chickens was changed to "laying mash," and crushed oyster shells were thrown into the yard. Eventually the membrane became covered by a hard shell and we had real eggs. Collecting them was fun. It was always a mystery to see how many you would gather.

As fall came, it was time to reduce the population and thus began the great chicken massacre. The railroad ties that we used to clean fish became chopping blocks for the birds. One by one they were caught and held by their feet while their heads were removed with a hatchet. They were then tossed into the garden where they would run a short distance and then flop over.

We picked up the chickens and brought them to a large pot of boiling water under the grape arbor. My mother and grandmother then dipped the headless birds into the water and plucked their feathers. It smelled horrible. Finally the birds were opened up and the guts were removed. Livers and gizzards were put into separate bowls. Sometimes eggs with no shells were discovered and saved for future use.

The massacre happened several times before winter set in. We ate a lot of chicken. In time, the population was reduced to a point where there were less than two dozen laying chickens kept. They met their maker one by one during the winter until the house was empty and ready for the next batch of peeps. Fried chicken, eggs, and clothing made from the feedsack cloth meant that we got as much out of the operation as was possible.

Keeping the chicken house clean was a job given to kids. Straw was thrown onto the floor and had to be removed once or twice a week. In the heat of summer it was awful. The ammonia produced by the chickens could curl your hair. We scraped it out with shovels and threw it onto the garden. Feeding and watering happened twice a day. We dumped feed into a large barrel kept just inside the door. Mice would get into it and would gorge themselves until they were unable to climb back out. You could see the feed moving as you dipped it out. It was like chasing an underground monster from a science fiction movie. You rarely saw the mouse, but rather the animated feed. Every so often we rolled the barrel outside to clean it and would find dead, dehydrated mice in the bottom.

It's been decades since I have been involved with chickens. A few years ago, as part of a water-quality study on the Potomac River, I toured a processing plant in Moorefield, West Virginia. Upon opening the door to the plant, I was greeted by the smell of steaming chicken feathers. This automated process didn't resemble our massacres at home, but the smell and the results were the same. It's much easier to go to the meat counter of the grocery store. I do not miss raising chickens.

MISS SHARFF'S CHICKENS

MANY OF OUR NEIGHBORS IN TOWN RAISED AT least a few chickens. The majority were fenced in but some were free range. Ours were always fenced in but not Miss Sharff's. She lived 100 yards from us in a house my sister now calls home.

Our coondog, Blue, was kept chained next to the barn. Partially bent nails held the chain to his dog house. Once in a while he would get loose and escape, and greet us at the back door with chain and collar still around his neck. Other times he'd take a stroll around the neighborhood accompanied by the sound of dragging chains.

Sometimes he went to visit Miss Sharff's house and proceeded to kill several of her chickens just for the fun of it. She had no trouble knowing who was responsible and neither did I. Blue would come home and greet me with feathers still stuck in his mouth.

I re-pounded the nails and attached him to the house just waiting for the inevitable. Miss Sharff would call my mother and tell her how many chickens were dead. I rounded up the same number from our pen and took them to her. She refused them, wanting cash instead. Her price was 50¢ per chicken. I believe it was never more than six or seven killed.

She might as well have asked for a million dollars. Where was I going to get three dollars? My parents paid. Not much was said until days later when it happened again. Blue was gone. He was given to one of my father's working buddies named Fletch. The irony is that not only does my sister now live in this house, but she is married to Fletch's son. I can't help thinking about this when I visit her.

⸺◦◦◦⸺

SHOOTING THE WATER TANK

MY MOTHER ALWAYS HAD A FEAR OF GUNS, AND we were continually reminded to be very careful with them. We owned shotguns and rifles for hunting. My Grandmother Engle slept with a pistol under her pillow. We had it after her death, but it was off-limits. My father did some hunting but it wasn't his passion. We all knew gun safety and never had a loaded firearm in the house.

Our drinking water came from a well. There was a water tank and pump beneath the kitchen counter, next to the sink. The holding tank had thick walls and held perhaps 10 gallons of pressurized water. On one occasion, my father was alone in the kitchen, cleaning a .22-caliber rifle. The rest of us were sitting in the living room when we suddenly heard a gunshot. My mother screamed, which was followed by complete silence. There wasn't a sound from my father, for reasons I will never know. Mom couldn't bring herself to get out of her chair and go to the kitchen, so she told me to go look. I can only imagine the scene she thought I was about to discover.

When I entered the kitchen my father was sitting at the end of the table with the rifle still in his hands. He said nothing but just stared at the cabinets across the room. They were painted white, like any good 1950s cabinets should have been. He got up from his chair, went to the cabinet, and opened the door to expose the pump and water tank. His shot had killed the water tank. He didn't actually kill the tank, but rather severely dented it with a .22 bullet. It wasn't leaking and we both stood silently looking at it.

His first words were that the gun wasn't loaded. I agree that it wasn't loaded *now*. He never did explain to us how the gun came to have a bullet in it while in the process of being cleaned. We never questioned anything, but could only imagine what would have happened if Deedle or I had been the one to kill the water tank.

CLEANING THE CISTERN

SEVERAL FEET FROM THE SIDE PORCH WAS OUR hand-dug well, some 10 feet deep. This was our primary source of drinking water. A hand-dug cistern was located in front of our kitchen window. From the top, both the well and cistern were just thick concrete slabs. While the well was supplied by groundwater, the cistern was filled with rainwater delivered through pipes leading from the roof downspouts. Cistern water was rarely used for drinking.

Eventually, a lot of debris would get into the cistern and we would be required to clean it out. First you had to pump out as much water as possible. Removing the concrete slab, you'd peer into a round underground chamber that was lined with concrete. It was about 10 feet deep and some 8 feet wide, very dark, cold, and mysterious. Into this abyss was placed a ladder.

On one occasion, my father was in the cistern putting the mud and slimy leaves into a bucket that I would pull up and dump into a wheelbarrow. This material was black, runny, smelly, heavy, and mixed with anything that had fallen into the spouting. When the wheelbarrow was full, it was pushed to the garden and dumped.

Apparently the wheelbarrow tire was old and weak and ready to explode, which it did with the sound of a shotgun blast directly above the opening to the cistern. It was loud above ground, but the reverberation down in the cistern must have been awful. In less than a second my father, who was six feet two inches tall, flew up the ladder and was standing beside me, totally out of breath. I don't know what he thought had happened but, this being during the Cold War, I can only imagine. It was the last time we cleaned the cistern together.

THE WELL FOOT VALVE
AND GLOVES

THERE WAS A TIME WHEN WE OWNED TWO OTHER houses in town and rented them to my uncles. These homes were not mansions and lacked central heat and indoor plumbing. One was a block duplex and had virtually no yard. Each side had a pitcher pump and kerosene stoves for heat. We never lived in this building. The other house was a single-family home we lived in until my grandmother in Charles Town died, forcing us to find a larger house for all the stuff she had.

This home also had a kerosene stove, and we installed an electric pump to get running water into the kitchen. The problem, though, was that it never really worked. It never held pressure because the foot valve located in the bottom of the well always failed. To repair this meant unhooking everything. The pump was located in a concrete-block pit several feet below ground, in the backyard. It was covered by a metal roof we could lift off. My fondest recollections of fixing the valve come from when it would break down during the winter, as it always seemed to do. We would have to pull foot after foot of heavy galvanized pipe out of the well to reach the foot valve.

The challenge was to keep the pipe from freezing while working on it. This was accomplished by using a blowtorch or two and constantly running them up and down the pipe as someone replaced the foot valve. The job took several people and a few hours.

On this job we used old torches filled with gasoline and pumped up to provide a hot flame. My father would let me wear his work gloves. When the gloves were new they had a fuzzy texture. This was removed by simply setting them on fire with the torch. They burned only a few seconds, but it was neat to be a human torch, if only briefly.

— ∞∞ —

HOT BRICKS

I COULDN'T BE WRITING THIS STORY ON A MORE appropriate day. Looking out my window in late January, I see the ground is covered with snow. The wind is blowing, rattling the storm windows as snow blows by. The air temperature is 19°F and the wind chill is 5°F. Tonight it will go down to near zero.

My childhood home was built between 1830 and 1835. It was large and in later years was heated by oil — but only downstairs. None of the upstairs bedrooms were heated. Three of the bedrooms had wood floors and the other two had linoleum. There were no storm windows. Drafts were strong enough to blow the curtains away from the windows, and ice would form on the inside of the panes. We didn't have a thermometer to tell us how cold it really was, and we probably didn't want to know. It was just plain cold.

Before the days of electric blankets and heating pads, there were hot-water bottles — red, flat, rubber water bottles with black plugs. Pour in the boiling water, cap it off, and take it to bed with you to keep your feet warm for a while. There were three children, three adults, and two hot-water bottles. You do the math.

We improvised with hot bricks. You'd place the bricks on the kerosene stove in the kitchen and heat them up. Mom sewed dishcloths into covers and wrapped them around the bricks to soften them slightly and keep them from burning us. The hot bricks went to bed with you and were used just like hot-water bottles, only not as soft.

They worked well for a short time but quickly lost their heat. After an hour or two they actually began to take heat *away* from you. If you woke up and felt this cold hard object at your feet, you kicked it out from under the covers. Today we're startled if a board creaks or an appliance turns on. Can you imagine the sound of five pounds of brick falling three feet onto a linoleum floor? Sometimes we would hear it hit the floor, but wouldn't give it any attention. We were snuggled under blankets and quilts in layers of pajamas, and had our clothing for the next morning flattened under our pillows, warming up.

My furnace just came on, and I need to put some more wood in the stove in the basement. I keep using a play on words from *Gone With The Wind*, saying, "As God is my witness, I'll never be *cold* again."

—∞∞∞—

THE SLOP JAR PUDDLE

U NTIL 1954 WE LIVED IN A HOUSE ALONG THE
road leading to North Mountain. On one side lived
the Browns and on the other, Miss Grabill. The Browns
were wonderful, but Miss Grabill was not. She lived in a
house that was large, in need of paint, and overgrown with
vegetation. It was a cross between the Addams Family
and Norman Bates houses. It was just plain frightening.
Miss Grabill was a small woman who wore long dresses
and black shoes, and ventured outside as little as possible.

Between her property and ours, alongside the highway,
was a low spot that filled with a few inches of water after
most rains. This was an ideal spot to play. I would make
stick boats and splash water by tossing in rocks. For some
reason this really bothered Miss Grabill. I was yards away
from her spooky house and not loud enough to be heard
or seen through the sprawling vegetation, yet she wanted
to stop me from playing in the puddle.

To this end she would come out the side door carrying
her porcelain slop jar. For those of you who don't know
what a slop jar is, it's a covered bucket used as a toilet in
houses lacking the convenience of indoor plumbing. Most

homes in town had at least one slop jar, and it would be carried out each day and dumped into the outhouse.

Miss Grabill decided to spoil my fun by coming around the side of her house carrying her slop jar. She removed the lid and without saying a word, poured its contents into the puddle before returning inside. She did this quite often, putting an end to my splashing and stick-boat floating.

Cod Liver Oil

WHAT CAN I SAY? IF YOU'VE NEVER TASTED IT, I can't begin to tell you how awful it is. We took it as a vitamin supplement. The tall rectangular brown bottle was kept in the refrigerator. We kids lined up and Mom filled a spoon with the thick, dark, oily-looking substance.

You opened your mouth and in it went. She made you swallow in her presence. I would stand there pinching my nose to avoid the smell and taste. After seeing that it was swallowed, she'd let you go. I would run towards the barn and spit and gag. No matter how long you delayed it, when you released your nose the smell and taste were still there.

Cod liver oil — what can I say? Today it could possibly be considered a form of child abuse.

—◦◦◦—

EASTERN FENCE LIZARDS

T HE HOUSE WE MOVED INTO IN 1954 WAS BUILT between the years of 1830 and 1835 by a Dr. Hartley. It was a large, log home that had been upgraded a little over the years and covered with German lap siding. The Beall family had lived there before us, and the yard and garden looked like a jungle. We spent several months getting the place ready before we were able to move in. The inside got a brand-new 1950s kitchen and the outside got cleaned.

My mother worked hard to defoliate the numerous shrubs and bushes, along with roses, that surrounded the house. One entrance to the kitchen had a small covered porch with a wooden floor. Under the porch, and running the entire length of the house, was a shallow concrete gutter that served to divert water away from the foundation. It was completely covered with bushes and served as the home for Eastern fence lizards. They are one of only two lizards native to this area. Today they are hard to find, but in 1954 they were everywhere.

My mother hated them and attacked them at every opportunity. After removing many of the bushes near the gutter, the lizard highway was exposed. She kept a very worn-down broom on the porch and would chase and smack them to death.

Families have protected themselves from being attacked by bears, bobcats, and other wild animals. Mom protected us from Eastern fence lizards. In fact, she may be single-handedly responsible for their extinction in Hedgesville.

Pets

MOST CHILDREN, AT SOME TIME IN THEIR LIVES, have a pet. There are inside pets, outside pets, wet pets, and pets that actually perform a useful function. We had all of the above and then some. My first recollection of a pet was my Grandmother McCarty's cat, Randy, who kept that name until he gave birth to kittens. Randy then became known as "Miranda."

Let's begin with cats. We always had cats. They were inside pets only if they ran inside when you opened the door. Some liked it inside and others only visited. If we didn't see them for a period of time it was no big deal. It seemed our cats were always having kittens. One time, a cat had her litter in the barn and they were attacked by skunks. The mother proceeded to carry the dead, half-eaten kittens down to the house, deposit them on our porch, and sit in the window sill until we came out to see her. That wasn't a good thing to see. We had Manx, or tailless, cats which we brought home from Charles Town. It was always interesting to see how many of their litter would have tails.

Dogs were treated entirely different from cats. Our dogs were outside dogs on the fringe of becoming hunting dogs. We had at various times a bluetick, beagle, collie, and some mutts referred to as "Heinz 57 Variety." There wasn't a deep love for them. They mostly hung around. A collie I had was shot at for chasing cattle. He eventually was poisoned by someone down the road who just didn't like dogs. It was no big deal. One dog got rabies and had to be killed, while another had fleas so bad that when washing it, the water turned red with blood. My mother did have several inside dogs almost until she died. They kept her company.

We went through the rabbit routine and had so many we couldn't give them away. I don't know why they never became a food source. We had several unfriendly squirrels. Perhaps our weirdest pets were de-scented skunks. Eating was their favorite pastime, and they got so big they could only waddle. My father put a leash on one and took it to the store. He got some strange looks. Once, while lying in bed, we heard something running in the attic. It turned out to be a non-pet skunk. As it couldn't be shot for fear it would spray, it was, instead, poisoned and died under the floor boards. My father scraped it onto a shovel, tossed it out the attic window, and it hit the ground and exploded.

We also had small pets, including fish, tadpoles, toads, an occasional snake — *hated by my mother* — and turtles. Box turtles were kept outside, but we did have a painted turtle that lived in a plastic pan complete with island and artificial palm tree. We had a small combination fish tank/ TV light. It would get so hot that it cooked the goldfish.

Our smallest pets were bugs. Lightning bugs were kept in jars until they rotted, becoming an oozy brown mixture in the bottom of the jar. Praying mantis eggs were a good find. I once placed a few egg cases on a shelf in the pantry where they hatched and crawled everywhere. I also caught cicadas and tied thread to their legs. They'd attempt to fly away as I held them. This provided entertainment for a few hours, until it was time to find a new one.

Pets were toys that ate and drank. They had no pedigrees or fancy names. I believe every child needs a pet to learn about responsibility and eventually, about separation. For us kids, pets were disposable family.

Dog Jumping

THIS STORY IS SHORT. THE HIGH SCHOOL WAS about half a mile from home and sat on top of a hill on the road to North Mountain. One day while playing somewhere in that area, I was cruising on my bike down the hill toward home, fast as I could go. The Snyders had a nasty dog that sat on their front porch. It would jump off and attack the wheels of cars as they went by. The dog even wore a muzzle over its mouth.

On this particular day it decided to attack me, or more precisely, my bike. It jumped off its porch and went right for my front wheel, bringing the bicycle to dead stop and throwing me over the handle bars. I continued to slide down the asphalt road for several feet. You can imagine the abrasions. My knees and elbows were torn up. Worst of all was the fact that I was wearing my first wristwatch, which was scattered into a million pieces all over the road.

My bike was only slightly damaged but the watch was a total loss. As I pushed the bike home, the dog returned to his position on the porch, waiting for his next victim. I only wish he had tried this after I began driving a car.

———

MILKING THE COW

NOBODY IN MY IMMEDIATE FAMILY OWNED A COW. For the first six years of my life, milk came from our neighbors, the Browns. Cows roamed freely in several fields around town. We shared the fields with them because in these fields were also our baseball diamonds. Cows were just big, grass-eating machines that got out of our way if we yelled and waved our hands. They only interfered by leaving cow pies everywhere.

A few cows grazed in the field behind my grandparents' house. My cousins and I got the brilliant idea to go milk one of them. Out the back door and over the fence we went with a Maxwell House coffee can. The cows weren't visible at first, but then one appeared at the far end of the field, walking — or rather, *charging* — from the barn and straight toward us. We knew something was wrong. Since the cow was between us and the safety of a fence several hundred yards away, we dashed across the field, jumped the fence, and ran into the woods — all of us except for one cousin, that is. She couldn't keep up with us, and decided to climb a less-than-stable tree while the rest of us escaped. We made it home and her father was sent back to rescue her.

What we didn't know was that the cow had given birth to a calf that morning and was extremely over-protective. We learned two things the hard way that day: all parents are protective, and we can't all run at the same speed.

GARDENING

HAVING A VEGETABLE GARDEN WAS SOMETHING almost everyone who was able to, did. Most homes had enough of a garden to provide fresh produce in season and plenty to preserve for winter. We were no exception. Our garden was an average-sized plot located at the back of our property, near the barn and chicken house. It was bordered by cherry trees and a rhubarb patch.

Neither the Runks nor the Pitzers used their gardens, so for several years they let us plant there too. Tomatoes, potatoes, corn, and beans were the staples. Nothing exotic was planted. They were always the same varieties because that is what the general store sold. I didn't know there were varieties other than Golden Bantam and Kenebec.

If we had a good year, we canned. One year our harvest was so plentiful that my parents decided to buy a freezer. Instead of one they bought two — both of which sat on the enclosed side porch until my mother's death, even though they had quit working years before.

Plowing the gardens was challenging. They were large enough to use a tractor, but it was tricky. We had no tiller or motorized garden equipment. The Hess family would plow your garden using a horse. Many townspeople found this method to be the best. A horse could make tight turns and thus didn't waste the corners of the garden. You could plow one day, disc the next, and plant the following day. Some residents actually turned their soil with a shovel. It took hours and hours, and I never saw any advantage to doing it that way. Tending the garden was everyone's job and was done by hand. Rows were laid out with a wheel hoe, which was also used to cultivate the plants. We dusted for bugs, but potato bugs received special treatment. We carried coffee cans filled with kerosene, picked potato bugs off the plants, and put them in the can. There were always bean beetles and most ears of corn had worms.

We were never self-sufficient, but we did grow a lot of our food. Gardening was just a part of the daily routine. When we had more than we could eat, we canned, froze, sold, or traded it. When we didn't, we either bought it or improvised. One thing is for sure — we were never hungry.

—⊗⊗⊗—

HULLING BEANS

B EANS WERE NEVER IN SHORT SUPPLY AT MY HOME. My uncle Charles always asked for soup beans first at all holiday meals. We grew bushels of green-, lima-, and bird-egg beans. After planting, cultivating, and picking, you got to hull them.

Hulling was done outdoors under a maple tree. All you needed was a pan for the beans and a bucket for the hulls. It was usually just a family affair and included my mother, grandmother, and us kids. Sometimes the neighbors joined in. We all sat in a swing hanging from the tree, in metal chairs, or on a wooden bench — sometimes for hours.

Your thumb would start to hurt from splitting the hull and scraping out the beans. There was a lot of enthusiasm in the beginning, but it quickly diminished as you watched the pan fill ever so slowly. We sometimes raced to fill our pans, but the more you looked at someone else's pan the less you hulled. One highlight was finding various colors of bird egg beans — some white, speckled, or almost pure purple. It really didn't matter as they all turned brown when cooked. If it was late in the season, some pods would be dry, hard, and shriveled. They were sharp and cut your hands.

You would find yourself looking at the communal basket where you got the beans to be hulled, wanting it to empty quickly. This setting was a time for family talk and the exchange of ideas. It usually ended up with a lecture due to too much casual kid-talk about things we had done.

The real kicker was that after bushels of picked beans and hours of work, the final collection of shelled beans just didn't seem enough. We did this several times each summer and tended to forget about the bad part until we were into the next picking. To top it off, most of us kids only liked green beans but ate the others to prove to ourselves it was worth all the hard work.

The Great Fireworks Disaster

THE DAYS BEFORE THE 4TH OF JULY MEANT A TRIP to Virginia to either Oak Grove or the Black Cat Tavern. These locations sold fireworks, all of which were illegal in West Virginia. We would come home with rockets, Roman candles, some exotic displays, and (of course) firecrackers, blockbusters, and cherry bombs. My brother and I managed to keep all of our fingers intact.

We sometimes had a 4th of July picnic with a fireworks display after dark. We would form a semi-circle around the launch site, sitting in metal lawn chairs only a few feet from the explosions. Sparklers, snakes, and bottle rockets were okay for younger children to handle. Fountains and Roman candles were taken care of by adults — usually by my father who somehow thought he was a pyrotechnic expert for one evening each year.

One display contained something called the "helicopter." It was placed on an upside-down wash tub and lit by my father. It was supposed to rise 10 to 15 feet, hover in the air, and then explode. It rose two to three inches and then flew in erratic circles right in front of us. Everyone fell off their chairs, hitting the ground as the helicopter spewed sparks only a foot above the ground. It then hit the house near the kitchen window. This was our last commercial display.

—∞∞∞—

GETTING THE CHRISTMAS TREE

F INDING THE FAMILY CHRISTMAS TREE WAS MY father's job. He would take us kids along with him, but the decision was his. There was no such thing as a tree lot, and artificial trees hadn't made it to Hedgesville yet. We jumped into our 1955 Chevy truck and headed for the woods. There weren't any black-and-red "NO TRESPASSING" signs and the fields were full of trees.

Finding the perfect tree could sometimes be a problem. God had planted and maintained the trees, not a tree farmer. They were mostly yellow or bull pine. They were long on smell but short on shape. We walked from one tree to the next, carrying our bow saw, and discussing the flaws we observed on each tree. By the process of elimination, we chose the tree with the fewest flaws, and down it came.

My father was the tree hunter and my mother the tree critic. Standing outside the kitchen door, my mother would survey our find. Most often she discovered flaws that we hadn't noticed. We'd lean that tree against the house, and head off to search for another. This process was sometimes repeated again and again until the side of our house became a forest of green.

Eventually one was chosen from among the many, and into the house it came. We placed the trunk into a bucket and placed rocks and bricks around it. Our tree never stood up straight, so a string was tied to its center and we nailed it to the wall. When it was as straight as we could get it, out came the strings of lights. My father began checking them around Thanksgiving. Remember — if one goes out, they all go out. I watched him spend hours trying to make the strand work. Then came the glass bulbs, along with the sound of several of them falling to the floor. A couple bulbs survived my childhood and we use them on our tree to this day. Now for the icicles. They were heavy, metal, and not anything like the translucent ones you find today. Icicles were most often used to fill in the gaps in our perfect tree. When completed, we stood back and admired our work.

This tree was lucky. It made it into our home and into our picture album. The trees left out alongside our house were either butchered for holiday greenery, or hauled up to the garden and burned in the spring. Our inside tree eventually met the same fate.

When our children lived at home, we went to tree farms and roamed in the cold until we found the perfect tree. Today our tree is an artificial one, and lives in the attic in a box until we bring it out after Thanksgiving. My son keeps reminding us that we have a plastic tree. It is a ritual with him and his family to go on the tree hunt, and my wife and I go along. I watch his family critique the trees much like we did. He straightens, adjusts, and ties the tree to make it stand with the best side facing out. I, on the other hand, place the appropriately colored limb into the correct slot, and my wife adjusts each branch. We string lights, hang bulbs, and add our memories to create the perfect tree.

CHRISTMAS

THE THREE BIG HOLIDAY CELEBRATIONS WERE divided between my mother and her two brothers. Uncle Charles and Aunt Frances hosted Thanksgiving dinner, and Uncle Cronie and Aunt Helen hosted Easter. Christmas was my mother's responsibility, mostly due to the fact that my grandmother lived with us after Granddad died. Throughout the year, our house was always a central location for visits. Uncle Cronie stopped by several times a week, and Uncle Charles usually visited Sunday afternoons. We lived only minutes from each other, but holiday dinners and parties made it an extra special time to see each other.

Christmas consisted of two events: a party Christmas Eve and a dinner Christmas Day. On Christmas Eve, the family would trickle in little-by-little, and by early in the evening we were all gathered. My grandmother always sat in her rocking chair by the living room window, taking in everything. Her hearing got progressively worse and we kids got progressively louder. My father wasn't the most sociable person. He often sat in the kitchen during most of the festivities.

Christmas Eve was the time when our family exchanged gifts. There was never a lot of money, but extra funds always seemed to be available to buy gifts at this time of the year. All of the adults bought gifts for each of the children from every family. What a wonderful idea from a kid's point of view! Mom served refreshments while the giftwrap flew, but she was already busy preparing for the next day and the big meal she would be hosting.

On Christmas Day, the relatives arrived, most wearing something new. The kids would bring their favorite new toy from Santa Claus. My grandmother's brother, Uncle Fred, would always come for Christmas dinner after he became a widower. He was a strange character who taught me how to hang wallpaper, but I'll leave Uncle Fred for the next story.

Our dining room table was large enough to seat well over a dozen people. It had so many leaves that we couldn't use them all. We would position the table diagonally in the room, extending it as far as possible, but that would accommodate only about half of the place settings we needed. Card tables and odd chairs were arranged in the living room to seat the rest of our guests. This was not a potluck dinner. Mom did it all, and she usually grabbed a bite while standing and refilling bowls. My aunts would gather in the kitchen to help her out.

No matter what was put on the table, my Uncle Charles would always ask for the soup beans. There was never a shortage of food to eat. The meal consisted of country ham, turkey, mashed potatoes, gravy, sweet potatoes, dressing, soup beans, green beans, sauerkraut (my father's favorite, along with anything covered in pepper), cranberry salad, coleslaw, corn, and rolls. Many different cookies, cakes, and fruit salad were served for dessert. There were always plenty of leftovers. We ate at noon and sometimes again later in the evening.

Christmas Eve was, and still remains, my favorite time of year. I have always liked the anticipation of what was to come more than the event itself. Mom kept the tradition alive as long as she could. When my grandmother died, the family drifted apart and my cousins began new traditions with their children. The Christmas Eve party also ended, but my wife immediately picked it up. My sister now hosts dinner on Christmas Day. It's not exactly the same, but it helps keep the family close. My cousins Carole and Steve, and their families, come each year. Uncle Charles's side of the family rarely attends, and we don't see them as often.

The Christmas Eve Open House has become my family's biggest annual event. Our children arrive in the evening, along with an ever-increasing number of grandchildren and great-grandchildren. We have extended our tradition to our circle of friends, increasing both the guest list *and* the fun. My wife cooks for several weeks in preparation. Our home is not nearly as large as my parents' house was, and we are crammed full on Christmas Eve. I find myself wishing we could have a bigger house for just one day a year. When the party is over and everyone has gone back to their homes, it takes several hours to wash dishes and clean up. My wife and I use this time to reflect, and remember how lucky we are to have our family, our friends, and the chance for everyone to get together for at least one night each year — however chaotic it can be.

My memories of Christmas are intentionally void of the mention of specific gifts. They weren't then, and aren't now, the main focus. In fact, I can only remember a few gifts, such as a bike, BB gun, radio, and typewriter. My father bought some electric trains at Joe the Motorist's Friend, which were sometimes placed under the tree. We visited Santa Claus at the Lace Store, and wrote lists that we left out with cookies and milk. The warm feeling of the holiday outlasted the temporary rush you got from a gift.

It's always been said that it's the *thought* that counts. This couldn't be more true, but now I think it's the *memory* that counts. The smell of the house, the piles of wrapping paper, the attention given to eager children while reading the assembly instructions for their new toys and searching desperately for batteries — these are with me each season.

FRED AND ETHEL

UNCLE FRED WAS MY GRANDMOTHER MCCARTY'S brother. He and his wife, Ethel, lived in Martinsburg for some time in an upstairs apartment, but he returned to live in Hedgesville when he became a widower. Uncle Fred seemed an unusual character, but his uniqueness was never explained to us kids. Aunt Ethel was a cook for Towers Restaurant, making pies and desserts. Uncle Fred did many things, including wallpapering and selling "antiques."

Uncle Fred dressed like someone out of a movie from the early 1940s. He always wore a hat and, except in summer, he wore a long overcoat as well. This may not sound like anything unusual, but Uncle Fred was just about as round as he was tall, and so was Aunt Ethel. He had no children and we were his closest family. He always returned to my mother's house for holidays.

When he moved back to Hedgesville, he lived in a house near Pitzer's pond. He had a rather odd friend, Johnny, who lived in Hagerstown, Maryland. Johnny was a frail little man who wore cowboy boots and thought he was an artist. He had a lisp and always laughed when he spoke. On one occasion, he brought a painting to my grandmother.

She had little interest in it but told him it looked good. He replied saying, "Miss Mary, you have it upside-down." She didn't realize that the painting was upside-down, even though it depicted a stream running through it.

Uncle Fred gave me two very useful gifts. First was teaching me how to hang wallpaper. The second was my first car. He owned a 1949 Studebaker that he sold to me for $50. I was only 15 years old and unable to drive it legally, but I still drove it to Martinsburg. It was jet black with suicide doors. My parents allowed me to drive it around the alleys in town even though it had no insurance and I had no license. I taught myself to drive with this car. When I turned 16, I sold it for $100 and bought a 1954 Ford, but that's another story.

PORCH SITTING

ALL THAT YOU NEEDED TO PORCH SIT WAS A PORCH, a few chairs, and nothing else to do. Our front porch was big enough to hold a glider and four to five rocking chairs. Every house in town was outfitted for porch sitting. At times it would just be kids sitting and planning our next adventure. Sometimes it would be adults taking a break.

Most often the porch contained a mixed cast of kids and adults. This was a time to exchange information and stories. We rocked, talked, and listened — sometimes for hours, and well into the night. We had no air conditioners, so outside was the coolest place to be. My grandmother talked to my mother and father as we listened. Sometimes we played games, but mostly we gossiped about those who rode past the house. Everyone would beep their horn, and we waved whether we knew them or not. Seeing someone in a vehicle usually evoked a new piece of information that had to be shared.

Visiting on others' porches was also a common practice. It was neat when neighbors came by because you always heard something new, or at least a different variation on the same theme. World politics was seldom the topic of our discussions. Rather, town news was the hot topic. I guess porch sitting was a forerunner of social networking.

—◦◦◦—

GRANDMOTHER'S BIRTHDAY GIFT

FOR SOME UNKNOWN REASON, MY BROTHER AND I decided to buy a birthday gift for my grandmother one year. The only problem was that we didn't have money. Between the two of us, we never had more than a few cents.

Poisal's Store had a small section of products suitable for gifts. We peered through the glass cabinet and chose a box of powder. In order to get it we would need help. We enlisted several friends and set off in search of money. Pop bottles were our prey. You got 2¢ for each one and 5¢ if you found the large ones, but they were rare. After a few hours of road-walking and collecting, we headed to the store to trade our glass for cash. When all was said and done, we had less than a dollar, but it was just enough money to buy the powder.

Proudly, the whole gang presented the powder to my grandmother. She accepted it with a surprised look on her face. I doubt if she ever used it, but it was the thought that counted, or so we were told. I still can't remember why it was so important to get her a gift that year, but we did. I'm sure she was more surprised by the gift than we were by the fact that we were actually able to purchase it.

—◦◦◦—

School

THE TOWN OF HEDGESVILLE HAD TWO SCHOOLS. First through sixth graders attended the elementary school, while seventh through twelfth graders attended a combined junior and senior high school. The elementary school teachers were local residents and all but one were female. They knew both you and your parents very well. Many attended our church and lived near my house.

Elementary school was nothing exceptional. We learned in spite of ourselves and received about as good a 1950s education as anyone could expect. There were plays and music concerts. I played Santa once and was in our version of "I Remember Mama," which was as far off-Broadway as you could get. We were even visited by a circus, complete with calliope, clowns, and elephants.

Going to seventh grade was a major part of growing up. There was a ceremony and sixth-grade students walked up the hill to the high school for a visit. We never realized how small we were until we got there. The students seemed so mature and we were so young. You fit in very quickly though. The principal, Mr. Kilmer, was a neighbor and was nicknamed "Sam Catchem."

The high school was built on a hill with several terraces below it where the athletic fields were situated. Sports were popular, especially basketball. I tried some, but wasn't very good. Shop classes were offered in spite of the fact that we had neither a shop *nor* tools. There were a few hundred students in all, and the high school served as our hub for social activities. There are many school stories to tell, with most of them coming beyond sixth grade.

WRITING THE DICTIONARY

PUNISHMENT IN ELEMENTARY SCHOOL INCLUDED no recess, a smack on the wrist with a ruler, standing in the corner, and ultimately a paddling. In the sixth grade we were introduced to a punishment more severe than all of these: writing the dictionary.

Sixth grade was about the time we were becoming aware of sex. Our teacher would walk around the classroom in her squeaky, crepe-soled shoes, and if she happened to say the word "but," we'd have to laugh. Her punishment for each offense was to assign us several pages of the dictionary to copy. This was awful as we were also to learn something while receiving this new, progressive form of punishment.

We became rather good at the task and developed some speed. We even tried to bank some pages for future use but she got wise to this and skipped around the book. I learned nothing from this except that you can put a lot of words on a page in the dictionary.

∞

FLAVORED STRAWS
AND STEWED TOMATOES

OUR ELEMENTARY SCHOOL CAFETERIA WAS RUN like a prison. Teachers who were not in charge of you in the classroom could give you orders in the cafeteria, and they seemed to love doing this. The meals must have been tolerable because none of them really stick out in my memory, except for milk and tomatoes.

When it came to food, you had no choice if you ate the cafeteria meal. The other option was to pack your own lunch. I did a little of both. We had no advanced menu given to us, so each day was a surprise.

I was never very fond of drinking milk and it was the only beverage served in the cafeteria. My mother bought flavored straws to counter this. There were two types:

chocolate and strawberry. When you drank milk through them the milk became flavored and the problem was solved.

For some reason we had a never-ending supply of stewed tomatoes. They were horrible, red, runny, seedy occupants of one compartment of the tray. The teachers, like prison guards, would circulate around the tables, watching you as you ate. You couldn't leave the cafeteria and play outside until they gave you permission.

They insisted you eat everything. If after many tries this failed, they insisted that you at least try everything. Stuffing your empty milk box with unwanted food rarely worked as they would often lift and shake the box. If you sat and stared at your tray for what seemed like forever, they would let you go with only a few minutes of lunchtime remaining for play.

My salvation finally arrived when our neighbors, Taddy and Effy, became school cooks. They would pass secret information over the fence to my mother warning her of upcoming menus. I was able to avoid the dreaded stewed tomatoes and actually have some recess after lunch to play.

—∞∞∞—

THE TREE HOUSE

MOST BOYS TRY THEIR HAND AT TREE HOUSE construction, and my brother and I were no exception. We were lucky enough to have a big maple tree growing between the barn and chicken house. Big would be an understatement. It would have taken several of us kids holding hands to circle its trunk. It hung over our property as well as the neighbor's, with horizontal limbs several feet around and large enough to be trees in their own right. They branched out about 10 feet above the ground and afforded the perfect platform for construction. One rather large limb extended over our neighbor's garage. Notches had been cut in the rafters to allow for the limb, but not for its growth. As the limb got bigger, the building got shorter.

We had no adult supervision and only minimal tools. What we lacked in expertise we made up for in volume of nails. We must have used 50 pounds of nails in that tree. Boards were nailed to the tree and used as a ladder. We nailed to the tree any wood we could find, creating several levels for our tree house. Rarely was anything cut to fit. It was nothing fancy, just platforms to sit on and a rope to haul things up.

There were no rules or a plan for the whole thing. We once decided to use the tree house as a base for our very own fire department. We had a wagon and several containers of water and just sat waiting for another fire disaster to happen in town. Mrs. Duke was kind enough to burn some weeds in her backyard, and we went there to oversee it. She thanked us and even served us refreshments. I think she just felt sorry for us and burned the leaves strictly for our benefit.

Tree houses are just fun. The building process is at the center, and you make things up as you go along. You learn cooperation and teamwork. There is a sort of freedom being above the ground in your own world. Some people try to recreate this feeling all their lives.

TELEVISION

TELEVISION WASN'T REALLY IMPORTANT DURING my early childhood. We got our first TV when I was about six years old. TV was on just a few hours each day, and we had only a few channels from Washington, D.C., and Baltimore, Maryland.

Our first set was a rectangular table model made of a black, plastic-like material. It was several times deeper than it was wide. The screen was only six or eight inches square. We had a thick glass lens that attached to the set to increase the viewing area. It distorted the picture, which was fuzzy to begin with.

I can only remember a few children's programs, most of which were local ones from Washington, D.C. Titles included "Captain Tug," "Ranger Hal," and "Pick Temple." There was also wrestling, "Amos and Andy," and news with Bryson Rash reporting. As I remember, the news lasted 15 minutes and was sponsored by Rams Head Ale. It's weird that this fact sticks in my head.

One kids' program I remember was "Winky Dink and You." The host would draw Winky in various situations, and throughout the show, you were asked to help him. I should say that you first had to send away to get a kit with crayons and a piece of plastic film to cover your TV screen. I never got this kit but figured my crayons would do just fine. When Winky needed a bridge, the artist would stop and allow the viewer time to go to their screen and draw in a bridge. When my parents found out what was happening, Winky received no more help from me.

Television wasn't the focal point for family life that it is today. We played outside and usually came in only to eat. We did have some TV dinners in later years but did not eat them in front of the TV. My favorite was the fish triangles with peas, carrots, and tater tots.

As we got older and TV programs became more varied, they slowly took root in our daily lives. We found ourselves spending much more time in front of the set and even scheduled things around it. My children would not have survived with the limited selections and times of viewing. How did we survive without cable?

<hr />

GHOSTS

EVER SEEN A GHOST? IF SO, DID YOU HAVE THE nerve to tell anyone? Was there a fear of ridicule or a fear that others would have an equally bizarre story to which you would have to listen? Ah ha! Perhaps I've gotten your attention. Let me share with you *my* ghost story. Read it if you dare.

Living in a house built in 1830, you become accustomed to creaking, cracking, and unexplainable sounds. This isn't what my story is about, as there isn't any sound involved in what happened — none at all. There is also no history of any tragic events ever having taken place in our house. The original house was built as part of a doctor's office and people had died in the house, but this was common.

Our house had five bedrooms, and I had used three of them at one time or another — it seems that we played musical bedrooms periodically. My story happened in the middle bedroom on the east side of the house. The back bedroom was over the kitchen and had been used by the kitchen help long before we moved in.

I was probably 12 or 13 at the time of this event. I had an old metal bed with a cedar chest at its foot. We had no TV or radio in our bedrooms, so when you went to bed, you went to bed. Sometimes sleep came quickly, and other times it didn't. On this particular night I noticed a faint, white, cloud-like object pass from the back bedroom into my room. It didn't come directly through the connecting door, but rather through the wall between the door and chimney. It was translucent and, although it had human-like form, it lacked any distinct features.

My eyes were immediately directed toward it, and I remember trying to sit up and yell. I was unable to do either. It floated a few feet, hovering over the cedar chest. It came forward over my feet and just floated there, becoming a little more dense and human-like.

There is no way of guessing how long this event lasted. Later, the apparition retreated back into the wall, following the same path of its arrival. The weird thing is that, after it disappeared, I was no longer scared or felt the need to yell for help. I never said anything about this to anyone at the time. This is a crucial part of the story. Years later I did talk about it with my wife, but just in passing conversation.

Many years later after my father had died and Mom continued to live in the house alone, she said in a matter-of-fact way, that the ghost had been back again last night. I asked her what she was talking about, and she told me a story of how a cloudy figure had come through the wall of the middle bedroom and hovered over the cedar chest at the bottom of *her* bed. It then moved over her feet and after some time went back through the wall.

You can imagine how I felt hearing this. We shared details of our encounters, and she said that this was not its first visit. She never said how many times it had happened, but from what she said there had been a good number of visits. We both agreed that we felt no harm and were not threatened in any way. We just went back to sleep.

I imagine that some of you might be thinking this never really happened. Perhaps we were just in that in-between state of being not fully awake, but not completely asleep. Regardless, doesn't it seem unusual that both my mother and I had such similar stories covering a span of many years? My wife thinks I'm crazy. Perhaps this is true, but how do you explain stories with so many parallels?

After mom passed away, I went through the house to clean up and prepare it for sale. When I got to the middle bedroom where I had met the ghost, I actually felt a little uneasy, almost to the point of being scared. I had never before had feelings like this in our home. It was a cold, chilling, hair-raising feeling. It may seem a little bit silly, but I actually looked around to see if I was being watched. As a child, this sort of thing should have scared the crap out of me, but it didn't. Now, as an adult, I felt uneasy and wanted to leave the house.

Mom always said she wanted for one of us kids to live in the house after she was gone. We all had homes and I think she probably knew this was not going to happen. We sold the property and another family lives there now. Perhaps in the future I will speak with them and see if they have had any similar encounters.

You can decide whether I am crazy or not. I don't spread this story around, maybe for the reasons I stated earlier. At my age, I don't care what other people think about me. In fact, I never have. Each one of us has to deal with what is real and what is not. I have had my mind made up for years. All that matters is what we keep and carry inside of us. This is my ghostly baggage.

———⊗⊗⊗———

ADVENTURES IN CHARLES TOWN

CHARLES TOWN WAS MY FATHER'S BIRTHPLACE, located about 25 miles from Hedgesville in Jefferson County, West Virginia. My grandmother lived there alone from 1948 to 1954 in a large white stucco home. We visited her several times a month by car and sometimes picked her up in Martinsburg when she arrived by bus.

Her house smelled old and musty, was rather dark, and was filled with antique furniture. I don't remember eating many meals there, but I do recall helping her make lady fingers. My grandparents owned several properties there that they rented. I was just old enough to be able to go with my father to do repairs on them.

In Charles Town, there was an extremely small dining establishment named Natalie's Tiny Kitchen. Natalie's was no larger than a bathroom and served food through a glass window. Right down the street lived a man who collected pop-bottle caps and kept them in barrels on his side porch. He must have had tens of thousands of them.

Aunt Daisy lived just a few blocks further. She and her husband had been missionaries in Africa. They returned with lots of bizarre souvenirs. She had trunks filled with elephant tusks, yards and yards of fabric, and wooden toothbrushes, to mention only a few.

As a widow, she lived alone and had rather peculiar ways. She never threw away anything. Her table had just enough empty space for her to put a plate. Piles of books and papers cluttered the table, along with food items covered in brown and green fuzz. She would just scrape off the fuzz and eat whatever was beneath. She did not have refrigeration in Africa and felt no need to use it at home.

My grandfather had several brothers and they owned a farm out on Route 51. No one lived in the farmhouse, so Aunt Daisy used it to store her African mementos along with other assorted antiques. This became a factor and led to a big fight when the property was sold. She was forced to buy back her personal property at a public auction that lasted several days. She sent individuals to bid and buy her items, and bring them back to her home and other places for storage. She refused to pay for any of them in person, as they were hers. Her relatives took her to court and she eventually won the case, but the ordeal hastened her death.

Aunt Daisy always wanted me to become a minister. To this end, she deposited $1,500 into a bank account with a letter stating it was for higher education. I have the letter, but have no idea where the money went as I never got it. She did give me a large, decrepit, chest of drawers. She said it was part of a set, the rest of which could be found in the White House. I never confirmed this, but antique dealers went nuts when they saw it. I had no idea what to do with it, so I sold it and used the money to purchase a 1962 Chevy. It served me well all through my college years, helping me get to class, graduate, and eventually become a teacher. I think Aunt Daisy would've been happy.

Another character was Sam Michaels. He lived on a farm several miles from town and was a close family friend, although I don't know why. He was a unique fellow and kept many exotic animals such as buffalo, albino deer, and peacocks. His home looked like a southern mansion with large columns on the front and many large windows in the stuccoed structure. The strange part of this story is that when he died, he left the property to Jefferson County with a stipulation that the animals be cared for until they died of old age. As a summer job, I worked for several years with the WV Department of Natural Resources, and one of my duties was to drop off feed for the creatures.

The animals eventually were shot, escaped, or died of old age. The property is now part of Jefferson County's park system and is the site of a major, semi-annual arts and craft festival. The house was also used as a movie set a few times. Sam had a friend who lived with him and remained in the house until the property was unsafe to inhabit.

A few miles down the road was the Duttrow farm. It was dilapidated but at one time had been very profitable. Lucy, the daughter, lived there along with her mother and father. She had been a classmate of my father, and the running joke was that she had a romantic interest in him. The Duttrows always had a gift for my father, or so it seemed. They usually gave him a carton of cigarettes that they'd retrieve from their chest freezer. I have no idea why they kept frozen cigarettes. We only had short visits to the Duttrow's farm as the family was either very eccentric or just crazy.

My father told me stories about Charles Town. Some of them seemed too strange to be true. One was about a cave containing an underground lake below the town that had been used for boating and even had a stage area for dances. Years later the newspaper reported about this. It was all true. Another story was of a drunken man who would climb the water tower to sober up. Another was about a man who lay on the train tracks and was dragged a distance by the train. He was retrieved in pieces. I'm sure Charles Town was, to my father, exactly what Hedgesville was to me.

⟨⟨⟨

HAIRCUTS

MY FIRST HAIRCUTS WERE GIVEN BY A BLACK man named George Thompson. We only knew him as "George the Barber." Being Hedgesville's only barber, George saw us several times each year, and was single-handedly responsible for keeping us looking respectable. His shop was painted gray and had a standard tin roof. The building it was situated in adjoined Dr. Grabill's dentist office, and both businesses had front porches with a tin roof that covered the sidewalk. This was the location where we kids would pitch pennies, especially on rainy days.

George's shop was just beyond the back corner of my yard, where a large yellow cherry tree and a crab apple tree grew. Our yard was enclosed by a wire fence, and right behind the cherry tree, it was smashed to the point where you could just step over it. This was one of our paths out of the yard, and how we got to the barber shop.

George's one-man shop consisted of two rooms which were separated by a curtain hanging in the doorway. The waiting area had gray metal lawn chairs, just like the ones many people had on their porches. The room where your hair was cut had just one chair. The shop was almost doctor-like with its tools and antiseptic smell. When we arrived, we would find George dressed in a traditional white barber coat. He was both a professional and a gentleman, and always greeted his customers as "Mr. so-and-so." He treated us kids just like the adults, which made us feel special.

For a kid, getting a haircut was a big thing. For most of the events in your life, you were usually accompanied by a parent. They controlled your clothing choices as well as your general appearance. Not so for the haircut. At the barber shop, it was just you and George. With money in hand and no parental guidance, you had unlimited choices to change your appearance — or at least you thought so.

There were pictures of hairstyles hanging on the wall, and George would ask me how I wanted mine cut. I don't think it really mattered how I responded. He knew it was going to be the usual shortening of the hair, so he began cutting. Maybe an unwritten agreement existed between George and my parents so that nothing strange would ever happen to my hair. With lowered ears, powder on your neck, and the smell of whatever it was that he splashed on you, you went home. My parents always gave my new style their seal of approval, saying that I looked much better now. I guess I did, but I didn't much care.

George eventually left Hedgesville and opened a shop in Martinsburg near the courthouse. Sounds like Mayberry, doesn't it? A succession of barbers followed and opened shops at different locations. Some even made "house calls," as my father had his hair cut in our kitchen by one of his friends who was training to be a barber. One barber left me with a lasting story. We called him the "Wading Butcher." On one occasion, I felt a warm sensation on my cheek as I walked home from his shop. I had a mole behind my ear and he had just cut it off. The warm sensation was blood. I had felt the sting of the liquid he put on, but he didn't feel it necessary to explain to me what had happened.

My parents never had a negative thing to say upon my return home from the barber. This was not the case, though, upon my return home from high school on a day in 1964. A female classmate had offered some of us what was to be a "Beatles" haircut, right there on front steps of the school. My father said it looked as if someone had put a bowl on my head and cut around it. He was almost right.

SCOUTING

I FIRST WANT TO THANK ALL THE ADULTS WHO took time to organize and supervise scouting events in Hedgesville, including my late mother, and many others. When we were Cub Scouts, several different parents served as den mothers. As we got older, the same core group of boys came under the direction of three primary leaders.

Being outdoors was already one of my preferred daily activities, so I didn't have to be talked into belonging to a club that offered me even more outdoor opportunities. Scouting, though, was so much more than being outside. It taught skills and forced you to think and act as a team. We advanced in rank and earned merit badges. The goal of Eagle was ahead of me, but seemed somehow unattainable.

Camping trips were at the top of the fun list. Equipment was minimal. I bought a sleeping bag with money I had saved in a school banking program. My mattress was a bulky, rolled-up glider pad replaced at some point by a leaky air mattress. I later acquired a canteen, mess kit, and backpack. Each scout had a uniform, of course. Our tents were a rag-tag collection of the pup or umbrella variety, mostly all donated by our leaders.

Each den needed cooking equipment costing about $20. As usual, a lack of funds fostered our creativity. To earn the money, we froze blocks of ice, bought a scraper, paper cups, and syrup, and sold snow cones. Most were sold to other kids hanging around waiting to play ball.

We attended several camporees each year. We did all of the traditional things and had time to play as well. I vividly remember a rainy morning when it was my turn to cook breakfast. A small campfire was smoldering just outside my tent. We had five eggs left for eight of us. I cracked them into a dirty, carbon-coated skillet, reached out, and set the pan on the fire — never leaving the tent. It was a race to see if the eggs would cook before the pan filled with rain. When they were done, I yelled, "Come and get it!" Somebody ate them, but not me. I wasn't about to get out of that tent.

The highlight of camping season was spending a week at Camp Rock Enon. I did this a few times. There, you had it all — the regimen of "Reveille" in the morning and "Taps" played from a loud speaker at night. You took your turn as "T.O." (table orderly) and tried to get away with everything possible, including trying to smoke cigarettes and playing practical jokes on each other. Sometimes we'd climb on top of picnic pavilions, where we'd sing and play guitars.

Permanent structures at the camp consisted of brown wooden buildings which smelled of creosote. They housed the mess hall, lodge, camp offices and store. Campers slept in heavy green canvas tents that were situated on wooden platforms and accommodated two metal cots. Inside our tents we read comic books, told stories, ate snacks, and sometimes even slept. Sound sleepers would sometimes awaken to find that both they and their cots had been carried outside.

At camp we earned merit badges by taking classes each day. There was a lake for swimming and boating. You had to take a test to determine your ability as a swimmer. You received a circular cardboard tag that you placed on a board indicating you were either in or out of the water. The color of the tag indicated your swimming status. I was classified a non-swimmer the first year, but quickly was upgraded the next, as no one wanted to be labeled a "non-swimmer." The test required swimming several legs between a dock and a floating platform. I quickly passed.

Another fun activity was using row boats and canoes on the lake in the evenings. Only swimmers could use canoes, so non-swimmers were stuck with row boats and had to be accompanied by a swimmer. This all became moot late at night when we would sneak down to the lake and "borrow" the boats, usually leaving them at the far side of the lake. You just had to do it.

The lake also offered us the opportunity to "gig" frogs. We'd attach knives to sticks and begin hunting. Someone would trap the frog with their hands, and then we'd strike with our makeshift weapons. Several human fingers were inadvertently cut as a result of this imprecise art. The risk, however, seemed worth the reward — fresh frogs cooked over a campfire. Of course, they tasted like chicken.

It was here at the lake where I was selected for the Order of the Arrow, or OA. This happened at a ceremony called "tapping out," held on the dam at the far end of the lake. All scouts stood in a row, as a person — standing in full Indian gear and holding a blazing torch — came across the lake in a boat. When he arrived at the shore, he disembarked and ran the full length of the group several times as we stood watching in silence. Those scouts chosen for the OA were singled out by a leader standing behind them holding a white handkerchief. You were not aware of this fact as they were several feet behind you, and we had strict instructions to keep our eyes forward. Suddenly you would get jerked out of line and pulled or dragged to the center of the dam. After all selections were made, you were led off to a site and received further instruction. This was quite an honor as only about a dozen scouts were selected from the hundred or so present.

In order to complete the process, you had to go through what was called "The Ordeal," held after regular camp season was over. It included being led into the woods blindfolded to spend the night alone in deep thought. You were awakened and led off to a worksite to perform a pre-determined task all day. This was all done in silence. If you were successful in completing everything, you were inducted at a campfire ceremony. You received a white sash with a red arrow and were given the secret admonition by the Indian chief. The ceremony ended with Indian dancing and a silent walk back to camp.

Boy Scout camp was a blast. It was the longest time I ever spent away from home. It was an opportunity to meet new people and do new activities. It was a time to learn new stories like the "Woman With the Golden Arm," and hear tales of the nudist camp that was supposedly located just over the hill. I got to see another scout attempt to create an ice cream float in his mouth. He took a large bite of ice cream followed by an ample swig of pop. Before he could swallow, someone told a funny joke. The boy began laughing, which made him gag, and also made the mixture come pouring out of his nose.

We pass the sign for Camp Rock Enon on Route 50 whenever we make trips to Romney, West Virginia. I'm always reminded of all the fun I had at camp, and I tell my wife that someday I'm going to visit there again. I still visualize how it looked and think of it every time I get a whiff of creosote.

PART TWO

AROUND TOWN

Poisal's Store

POISAL'S STORE — RUN BY JIM POISAL, HIS SONS, and Robert Duke — was the only store in town. It was a general store in the purest sense — a real 1950s super store. It occupied one corner of the intersection at the center of town. Outside was a gas pump. There were two large windows and between them a single front door. Each new customer's arrival was unofficially announced by the slamming of the screen door.

One step up and you entered the store and stood on its wooden floor. The floor was often covered with green granules used to put oil into the wood. It had a distinct smell not duplicated today. The main part of the store was only about 40 feet square, but the attached feed and hardware section was slightly larger.

The store had everything you needed. On the left by a window was the loafing area composed of a bench and one metal lawn chair. Over the chair hung a Dr. Grabo pipe display. The area was separated from the rest of the store by the pop and ice cream cases, which served as overflow seating. Immediately behind the front door was a wooden barrel that contained salt fish, and on the other side of the door was a rack containing rolls of oil cloth.

Just inside the front door was the clerk area. The cash register sat in the center, flanked by upright glass panels, forming a U-shaped configuration. Penny candy was on the left side and candy bars were on the right. Wide wooden counters extended back some five or six feet on each side. Standing just opposite the cash register was a large metal cabinet that held the charge slips. This was used more than the register. Since money was scarce, charging was common, and most folks in town kept a tab. On Fridays, my father would cash his paycheck at the store and pay our bill. Sometimes he would even have money left over.

At the front of the store on the left, just behind the pop and ice cream cases, were bins of fresh vegetables, and a clothing section. Blue jeans, work clothes, socks, shoes and underwear were the main offerings. The center section of the store contained canned food and dry goods. There was not the selection we have today, but it was enough. There was even a cabinet at the end of one aisle where you could buy loose cookies and crackers. Imagine trying to buy just one Oreo today.

On the right side was the notions and toiletries section. There were cases filled with thread, needles, and buttons, along with powder and perfume. One of the front cases was used to display holiday items at Christmas. It was in Poisal's Store where I got my first 45 rpm record. It was a promotional item attached to a bag of potato chips.

Across the back of the store was the frozen-food and meat section. There was a large, white, walk-in freezer with a thick wooden door on the front. It had a window and you could see meat hanging inside. The center back area contained a meat case and butcher block. There were no pre-packaged meats and very little meat was on display. You told the clerk what you wanted, and they cut and weighed it for you. You even purchased hot dogs individually. In the far back corner of the store was the ammunition section where you could purchase shotgun shells by the piece.

Stepping down a step and through an opening in the wall put you into an adjoining building where hardware and feed were sold. Nails were stored in kegs, bolts were found in boxes, while bags of feed took up most of the floor space. When I was sent there to get chicken feed, I was instructed as to which color feed sack to bring home. We emptied the chicken feed into barrels, and the sacks were washed and turned into aprons, towels, curtains, and even a shirt or skirt.

This was our store. It was a one-stop shopping experience, much like department stores are today. Parking problems were nonexistent since we walked to the store. We rarely had to wait in a line. You never encountered an unfamiliar checkout clerk, because that same clerk did everything from cutting your meat to working the cash register. It also helped that the clerk was your neighbor, too. We left the store happy, as it was a good experience. This is not always the case today.

GRACE'S TOWN SPRING LUNCH

LOCATED ACROSS THE STREET FROM THE TOWN spring was the only restaurant in town. We called it "Grace's" after its owner. It was a true greasy spoon.

Grace's was a small structure adjoining the Albright's house, and was furnished with enough ice cream tables and chairs to seat about a dozen people. It served only sandwiches, fries, chips, sodas, and ice cream — nothing fancy. Submarine sandwiches were the specialty, but we called them "burp burgers."

Grace's was the local hangout for teens and preteens. In later years the so-called "old folks" loafed there, and both the ownership and the menu changed. In one corner was a jukebox with all the favorites from country to rock and roll. For some reason "Silver Threads and Golden Needles" and "King of the Road" just went through my head.

The real attraction — a pinball machine — was situated in a corner by itself and was our one-and-only source of gambling. A nickel got you a play of five balls, but you could add more change to increase your odds of winning. The cool guys never played just one nickel, and they kept their stash of coins on top of the glass above the flippers.

Playing pinball required concentration, so others could watch, but talking was discouraged. Looming over your head was the possibility of putting too much "English" on the machine. This would result in the dreaded word "TILT" appearing across the screen, and your game automatically ending. Avoiding this was a fine art. If you lost, you either walked away mumbling or, if Grace wasn't around, you'd kick one of the machine's legs. Sometimes it also received a hard push into the wall, followed by a hasty retreat.

You never made money from the beast, but if you won, it would give you free games to continue playing — or at least that's how it was supposed to be. If you got 20 free games, you could illegally cash them in and receive a dollar. It could become a habit instead of just a pastime. Once, when I returned home from Boy Scout camp, I discovered that my collection of buffalo nickels was missing. I can't prove it, but I think they were fed to the beast.

The restaurant closed years ago and is now owned by the Catholic Church. If I were Catholic and went there for church, it would be impossible to think of it as a sacred place, considering its past. Who says you can't make a silk purse out of a sow's ear? They made a church out of Grace's and Grace made burp burgers.

—∞∞∞—

THE BIG FIRE

IN NOVEMBER OF 1957 WE WERE LIVING IN THE house we kept until my mother's death, but still owned the one next to Miss Grabill. It was a cold and very windy evening. I don't know the exact details of how we were informed, but the word "Fire!" was yelled repeatedly. We ran out into the side yard and saw an orange glow in the sky to the north. The smell of smoke was heavy in the air.

A fire was blazing at the top of the hill about halfway to the high school. We ran toward it and just stared. It looked as if everything in that area was burning. I don't know where or how it originated, but both the Grabill house and even larger Ellis house next door were totally consumed in flames. Both homes were on the west side of the road, and we still owned the house adjacent to them. The flames were so big and the wind so strong that houses across the road had been set on fire as well.

A big problem was that Hedgesville only had a fledgling volunteer fire department. The №5 Fire Company located 10 miles away in Martinsburg always came to our rescue eventually. My aunt, uncle, and their twin daughters were living beside Miss Grabill. Uncle Charles was out hunting that evening. My father ran to their house and, using just a garden hose, sprayed water on the side of the house facing the fire. Others worked on the homes across the road.

Thinking this was going to be the end of Hedgesville, my mother gathered us kids together back at our house to prepare for an escape. The № 5 Fire Company arrived and was immediately put to the test. With no public water and the truck having a limited supply, lines were run to Brown's pond and pumped by the truck.

After some time, the resourcefulness and persistence of the town folks and fire company paid off and the fires were extinguished. The Ellis and Grabill homes were a total loss. Four houses across the road were badly damaged and two were later leveled. Our home had curled shingles but was still standing. This was a result of both my father's work, and the fact that the wind was blowing across the road and not sideways. This terrible night led to efforts to bolster our fire department and improve on our 1941 Mack pumper.

Some things stick with you for life. For me it is the big fire. I love fall with its crisp nights and a hint of smoke in the air, but I really dislike the wind. My wife has heard me say this on many occasions. Cold winter nights with howling wind always trigger a very vivid memory of the big fire.

THE INDIAN GRAVE

IT SOUNDS LIKE SOMETHING FROM *THE ADVENTURES of Tom Sawyer,* but we really were told to stay away from an Indian grave. The grave was located on the ground level of a barn that was used both for storage, and later as a residence for a town character named Harry.

The grave site was essentially a mound of dirt about six feet long and a foot high. Nobody ever provided details to us kids regarding the person supposedly buried there, or why a barn had been constructed over an Indian grave in the first place. I saw the site a few times, but only in the daylight. The building was pitch black after dark, and even in the daytime everything in the barn appeared gray. The grave was never used for dares or teasing. We didn't force anyone to go inside the barn, and there was certainly no invitation to visit. We played all around the barn in the daytime and at night, but going inside was a completely different story. Perhaps that was due to its tenant, Harry.

I don't know the circumstances that forced him to live in a barn, but I can assure you that Harry was as much a deterrent for entering the barn as was the grave. Grizzly, partially unshaven, and clad in bib overalls, he would sit next to one of the large, slightly opened barn doors. If we ventured into the barn to see the grave, we did so quietly because he slept on the level just above. He had a double-barreled shotgun, which I acquired almost 50 years ago.

The barn, the mound, and a couple of nearby buildings burned down in a fire which also caused damage to the adjacent Episcopal Church. I have been past the site a few times and can see only level ground. I wonder, do the residents now living near it even know what might be in their backyards? In later years I talked about this grave with the lady whose family had owned the barn. She knew nothing of it. As I look back, it makes no sense to build a barn over an Indian grave or bury an Indian under a barn. I now believe this was one of the best scams ever played on us kids. A scary story, a grizzly old man, and a pile of dirt kept us out of the barn. I'll never know the truth.

There are several interesting twists to this story. One of the eateries at our local mall had become a loafing place for some of the guys from Hedgesville. I would occasionally stop by and talk, especially with Boo. One day when I stopped in to ask him a question, he introduced me to the man sitting next to him. I didn't catch his name at first, but he talked about things in Hedgesville when he was young.

In the course of the conversation I learned he was Harry's son. I told him I had something I believe once belonged to his father.

I explained how about 50 years ago I had traded a pack of firecrackers for a shotgun which I was told had once belonged to Harry. The son remembered it and was amazed that I owned the gun — now more than 100 years old. The other twist is that after his father purchased the gun, he needed money during the Depression, so he sold it for $3. Later he needed a gun and went to buy a used one, only to discover it was the same gun he had sold a few years earlier.

I asked Harry's son to wait there a few minutes. I went home, got his dad's gun, and returned to the eatery. We went to the parking lot and I gave him the shotgun in the same condition as I received it, having never fired it myself. He said he thought he had a photo of his dad holding this shotgun, and he seemed happy to have it back in his family.

He thanked me again and each of us drove home. I felt happy that the shotgun had come home for a third time. I don't know how much Harry had originally paid for it. What I do know is that it was once sold for $3, and then traded for a package of firecrackers, but finally returned home for a handshake.

— ◆◆◆ —

Kate's Hollow

IT WAS ONLY A SHORT WALK IN ANY DIRECTION from my house to an open field or to the woods. There weren't any housing developments at this time, and when the few short streets making up Hedgesville ran out, there you were. My favorite location was Kate's Hollow. A hollow is simply a narrow valley between two mountains or hills. This hollow meandered several miles until it reached Back Creek. Miller's house and an unpainted, dilapidated barn marked the location where the dirt road ended and the path to Kate's Hollow began.

I don't know if many other families were as familiar with Kate's Hollow as mine was. Mom's family had lived on the Grabill Farm along Back Creek in the 1930s, and she and her brothers walked to school using the same path we used. My grandparents' back door was only a few hundred yards across a field from the entrance to Kate's Hollow.

My great-grandparents once lived in the hollow in a house that has since vanished. Before my Uncle Cronie's death, he led some of my family to the location where he believed the house had stood. He finally found it, but all that remained were pieces of slate, flat stones, and a couple of old pots and pans. I carried several stones back home. I had walked past this spot many times when I was a kid, but only noticed a spring and not the remains of a house.

On Sundays, back when my Grandfather McCarty was alive, the whole family would get together at their house for dinner in the afternoon. Grandma McCarty would serve us all lunch and iced tea. I specifically remember the big, white, porcelain pan she used for brewing tea, stained yellow from the groundwater's high sulfur content. After lunch, the entire family would head off for a walk down to Kate's Hollow. It's funny how these days, I can't remember where I put a tool in my workshop, but I can still visualize several miles of a trail I walked some 50 years ago.

The walk was always a slow one, and my aunts, uncles, cousins, and parents enjoyed all the sights along the way. The trail began on a path bordered by an abandoned field grown up on one side with wild berry vines. This slowly gave way to dense woods rich in undergrowth. The trail followed a stream all the way to Back Creek. The hollow was filled with large trees, and being surrounded by hills, received little direct sunlight. Ferns and moss thrived in this dark and damp environment and were abundant year-round. Skunk cabbage and May apples grew in springtime.

The path not only followed, but also crossed the stream at least a dozen times. In fall, the leaves would get several feet thick in places. We loved to kick them as we ran ahead, and we'd cover ourselves in them to scare the adults. The path would widen in places and then become very narrow. This was especially true as you passed Kate's Rock. Little is known of Kate, but rumor has it that she once lived in the hollow with her two sisters. No one had lived in the hollow for years, and only fragments remain of what had once been homesteads, most recognizable only by the presence of a few very large trees and access to a spring. Kate, however, as the namesake of the hollow, had a living presence in the minds of us kids because of stories the adults had told us.

A large outcropping of rocks, called Kate's Rock, came very close to the stream, making the path only 18 inches wide at that point. In order to pass by, you had to grab onto the rock, which rose at an angle toward the stream and hung over our heads. Adults told us that when Kate had once lived in the hollow, someone had cut off her head. It was said that she sat on the rocks — with her head held under her arm and a pipe still in her mouth — watching everyone who walked by. With this vision in our minds, we would always pass Kate's Rock as quickly as possible.

Water was an intricate part of the hollow, and many springs along the path merged to form a wider stream that headed to the creek. We used these springs for drinking, and regularly cleaned the leaves from them and arranged rocks around them. We drank the water with our hands, or created cups by removing the plastic covering from a pack of cigarettes. We ate raspberries in spring, and tea berries in summer. We always carried something to snack on. I remember having rolls of Necco Wafers, which my cousins and I called "energy pills." We needed them for the return trip, as it was all uphill. You really couldn't get lost on the walk. All you had to do was follow the stream until you came to the creek.

When you reached Back Creek, there wasn't an opening into a field or clearing. Trees continued right up to its bank. The creek became wide here, slowing down and calming the water. On the far side, rocks formed a partial dam and a beach-like area of small stones lay in between the deep water and the riffle. Here we fished and played in the water. In later years, some friends and I climbed the hill near the creek and piled up rocks to form a fort that overlooked the creek. We spent hours there. If we had sodas, they were kept cool in the stream. Hot dogs were sometimes roasted on sticks. We collected box turtles we found along the way, brought some home, and put them in a spring behind my grandparents' house. We carved names and dates into the underside of the turtles, always hoping to find them at a later time.

Kate's Hollow seemed to have it all. We fished, hunted, camped, and gathered things to bring home. There were lots of wildflowers and some are growing in my yard today, along with some hemlock trees. The beautiful thing about Kate's Hollow was the quiet and isolation you experienced there. It was all woods with no houses, roads, or people. We didn't care who owned the hollow, and you couldn't find a single "KEEP OUT" sign. It was our wilderness, and being there felt as if we were a million miles away from everything. This feeling changed though, when Hedgesville got a fire station. Every Saturday at noon the siren would be tested, and this could be heard from a great distance, even from down in Kate's Hollow.

My Grandfather McCarty knew the hollow well. He could walk out the back door, pass the hog pen, cross a field, and be there. He spent his last living moments in the hollow. He had gone hunting the first day of squirrel season in 1956 and never returned home. Instead, he was found sitting on a log with his shotgun lying across his lap, dead from an apparent heart attack. My father brought his body from the woods in his truck, as there was no good road for the hearse to use. It was sad to see him gone. Rarely, though, do people end up leaving this world so peacefully.

I guess all of these things helped me form a bond with this area that others in the town didn't have. I have always been drawn to nature, water, and the woods. My family's association with the area and its varied offerings make it a place I think about and visit occasionally. As Hedgesville grows, new brick and vinyl houses are being built near the path's entrance, removing the undergrowth in the process. Some of the new residents there look strangely at me as I pass their homes on the way to the hollow. Some have even questioned why I am walking there in the first place.

On my last trip there with my Uncle Cronie, when we searched for the foundation of my great-grandparents' house, shots were fired over our heads. We didn't see the marksman, but knew the direction of the fire was from one of the new homes on the hilltop. Minutes later a man and woman appeared a few yards away, staring at us. They asked us what we were doing there. I told them we were looking for the foundation of a very old house. They didn't buy it.

They explained how strangers had been seen digging for Civil War artifacts. Neighbors had warned them that a group of suspicious people were roaming the area. I knew we didn't look too good, but this seemed a stretch. Seeing that this was going nowhere, I asked them if they owned the ground we were standing on. I knew they didn't. They hemmed and hawed and said their house was up the hill in a new development. I attempted to give them the Reader's Digest version of what the area meant to us. They just stood and listened. To them, it didn't mean much. I told them to have a nice day and then watched as they backed away.

As you get older, you realize how much larger your adult world is and how much smaller the world of your childhood has become. Although Kate's Hollow is still the exact same distance to the creek along the stream, and springs can still be found along the dark, leaf-covered path, its isolation is rapidly disappearing. With the rush to leave large cities and move to the country, many people see Hedgesville as a great place to live, and housing is now encroaching on our little hollow. The sounds of new construction combined with the beeping of bulldozers at a nearby landfill, only serve to reinforce the fact that the days of Kate's Hollow, as I remember it, are numbered.

THE TOWN SPRING

HEDGESVILLE HAD A TOWN SPRING LOCATED JUST down the road from my house, and across from the future location of the town fire hall. It was situated on a small grassy plot and was bordered by State Route 9 and an alley. The spring house was built half below ground, and was about a 20- by 20-foot, square building. The roof was metal and all of the exposed wood was painted white. The above-ground portion was enclosed in screen, and there were two screen doors for entry. Several steps down into the building was a huge concrete square in the center with a walkway all around it, built up to the level of the ground outside. In the center of this massive concrete structure was a hand pump. It was always a cool and shady place, so we would hang out there on hot summer days.

Next to the town spring building was a pool of water several feet around and lined with large rocks. The water surfacing there was only a foot deep and came from the same source as our drinking water just a few feet away. The pool was a great place to catch frogs, crayfish, and salamanders. It was also a wonderful place to "borrow" minnows, or *minnies*, as we liked to call them. Minnies took time to catch and were great bait for bass. Fishermen collected large quantities of them, and kept them in the little pool, submerged in wooden boxes with tin sides and a locked door on top, ready at a moment's notice.

For us kids, it was a miniature fishing trip whenever we visited the pool. Minnies would escape the boxes and we would chase them with our hands. Catching one was the ultimate trophy. A shiner in a can was a thing to behold. Just having it was its own reward. When I was a small child, I didn't fish with them, but rather kept them in a can until they eventually died. We kids had a favorite secret place to store our minnies. Our general store, Poisal's Store, was just a block away from our minnie pool, and shared an alley bordering the town spring. The store had a chimney with two metal clean-out doors near its base. We would keep our cans of minnies just inside the clean-out doors, probably so our parents wouldn't find them dead around the house. Perhaps it was also because we didn't want to get caught with the evidence.

Now, as to the real purpose of this spring: it provided drinking water for the early settlers and early town folk. Hedgesville's residents typically got their drinking water either from a hand-dug well, or from the town spring.

Every well in town tapped into the same water table as the town spring, so if your well-water became contaminated, you could bet the town spring water was, too. Outhouses and septic systems were not inspected at this time, and many were located in close proximity to our wells. Guess what? The town had an epidemic of hepatitis, which was spread by our drinking water. About two-thirds of the town folk became hospitalized over a period of several months. If you have not had hepatitis, be thankful. It causes extreme weight loss, but not without a high cost.

Most towns were originally built around water sources, and Hedgesville was no exception. The town spring still stands, but I do not believe anyone uses the water. Public water and sewer eliminated many of the dangers that once threatened the health of the community. The minnie pool is now gone, unfortunately. It is no longer considered safe to have open pools of water where young children could fall in and perhaps drown. When I was a kid, however, the pool itself never posed any danger. The *real* danger was getting caught with someone else's minnies.

———◦∞∞◦———

North Mountain Brick Plant

Northern mountain brick plant was the only industry near Hedgesville, and was located several miles from town, along the B&O railroad tracks. Bricks were fired by hand in coal-fueled, beehive kilns. The plant employed several dozen people from the community.

I never knew my father to have worked any other job than this one when I was a child. He drove a forklift and unloaded bricks from the kilns and onto trucks and rail cars. He did what was called "piecework"— being paid for the job done and not by the hour — and his pay was not very good. Sometimes he would work all day, but usually he was home by early afternoon.

It was an extremely dusty and dirty place, and the kilns were unbelievably hot. A small train hauled clay from the pit to the pug mill, where it was formed into bricks, which were then prepared for firing. Baking the bricks took a few days and required around-the-clock attention. Several men watched the bricks at night, staying awake by drinking "RWL"— a liquor for which we never knew the full name, but decided the abbreviation stood for "run, walk, and lie down." It was cheap, but powerful.

As a child, I didn't think much about the brick plant or about the work my father did. I wasn't taken there often and it was not discussed much at home. The only reason I know it didn't pay very well was because on Fridays, after my father cashed his paycheck and paid our bill at Poisal's Store, I'd overhear him telling my mother that he wasn't able to pay in full that week.

The brick plant had just one employee perk: an annual family picnic. Usually held at the 4-H camp, it was a day-long event. We went early, however, as things often got out-of-hand as the day progressed. We could enjoy all of the food and pop we wanted. There wasn't much competition for these items because the main attraction was free beer. Employees could drink all the beer they wanted, and often consumed much more than they needed. Horseshoes were pitched as beer was guzzled. Arguments would erupt and people got hit. No big deal — they just drank some more.

We could also take food home with us, so we usually grabbed some pop and candy before we left. Even a beer or two came home, although nobody drank at our house. Mom said that the doctor told her she could drink a beer on occasion to keep her kidneys working. I don't think she ever did. The beer just got shoved to the back of the fridge.

I thought of working at the brick plant one summer. My father took me to see the manager, Lee Crowell, who walked me down to a kiln that had recently been opened. A fan the size of an aircraft engine roared with about the same volume. You could not hear much, but you certainly could feel the heat. Mr. Crowell said the kiln was ready to be emptied, and if I was hired, that this task would be mine. I returned home and began looking for a different job.

My father worked at the brick plant for more than 20 years. There had been a few strikes during that time, with the workers gaining some extra compensation, but the last strike was the end of the plant. The owner closed the doors and it never reopened. Unemployment benefits didn't last long, so my father searched for a new job. He found work at the Corning Glass plant in Martinsburg, but it lasted only a short time as he burned his hands badly while working on the line. He eventually got a safer, better-paying job at a newly opened General Motors parts plant. It was evident that our family's finances had improved when he showed up at the house my wife and I were renting, driving a new, baby-blue Malibu. Although I wouldn't be enjoying the financial benefits of his new job, I was glad that life would be much better for Dad, Mom, and my sister.

After closing, the plant sat for many years and began to just crumble away. The property was eventually sold and everything bulldozed flat. The site, situated adjacent to Kate's Hollow, now serves as a landfill, and the sounds of the equipment used to haul, dump, and bury our county's trash can now be heard from a place we once prized for its solitude. The only clue of the brick plant's prior existence is the manager's house at the entrance to the landfill, and the cut hillside where clay was removed. I can visualize the red brick kilns, the small white wooden office building, and the overhead train tracks leading to the pit, even though all of these are long gone. The only tangible evidence I have is a brick in the basement with "NORTH MOUNTAIN BRICK" stamped on its side.

I now serve on the board of directors for Martinsburg-Berkeley County Parks and Recreation. In 2009, the owners of the former brick plant decided to donate a large portion of the property to the park system. It seems that things have again come full circle. In the future, I will walk the brick yard again, visualizing where things once stood.

ALLENSVILLE FORD

W HENEVER YOU CROSSED BACK CREEK BELOW North Mountain, you used the ford — just like in the cowboy movies when horse-drawn wagons crossed a shallow part of the stream. We did the same thing in our cars and trucks. There was no bridge. The water was wide and shallow — usually 12 to 18 inches deep. If it was too deep, you didn't cross. You used common sense.

Tilhance Creek entered Back Creek at Allensville Ford and the fishing there was good. You could also drive your vehicle into the creek, open the door, and get out to wash your car. We kids played as our parents did this. We swam in the deeper areas, floated on tubes, or fished upstream. Locals were drawn here to drink and loaf. Many workers from the brick plant escaped here to have refreshments as it was only a short distance from their work. In the spring, people would net or dip suckers where the creeks joined.

A low-water bridge was built there in later years, sitting above the water by only a few feet. It was made of concrete with metal culverts running through it to transport water. Low-water bridges typically have no railings on the sides — just small, concrete curbs running the length of them on each side. When the creek was high, water could easily run over the bridge, so signs were posted to warn motorists not to attempt to cross in these conditions. Regardless, one day while fishing with my uncle when the water was high, we attempted to cross the bridge in an old station wagon. The water moved with such force that it pushed the car toward the edge of the bridge. Thankfully, we made it to the other side. We were very lucky and never tried this feat again.

Several years ago, on Christmas Day, a local family was returning home after dark. The water was high, but they ignored the warning sign and drove onto the bridge. The bridge's construction had created a deep hole on its lower side. When water is covering the bridge, water in that hole is about eight feet deep. As the family began to cross, their car was swept over the edge of the bridge, flipped upside down, and sank right into the hole. The entire family died, with some time passing before the body of one of their small children was found quite a distance downstream.

Despite its handful of tragedies, Allensville Ford was always a fun place to play and enjoy the water. Swimming through the bridge's culverts was a popular sport, but not too smart when you think about it. Rusty, corrugated metal pipes with exposed bolts and jagged edges provided an accident waiting to happen. I never tried floating through the culverts, but witnessed many individuals who did. My grandchildren once suggested they would like to try it, but I made sure this never happened. This feat later became an impossible one, however, when the original, low-water bridge was destroyed, and replaced with a real bridge.

I still take my grandchildren to Allensville Ford several times a year. We enjoy playing in the water, and collecting fossils and stones — many just right for skipping. One of our grandsons, I remember, spent hours one day trying to create a dam with the stones. We still begin our boat and canoe trips there in the shallow water, traveling upstream to calmer, deeper water, where we fish and swim. The place looks entirely different, except in my memory.

THE POLKA DOT

I BELIEVE IT WAS OFFICIALLY CALLED THE NORTH Mountain Tavern, but we all knew it as The Polka Dot. Several miles from my house and very close to the brick plant, this red-tile tavern was about a room-and-a-half big, and just several feet from the road. A few tables and chairs, along with a bowling game, filled the interior. Outside was space for only a couple of vehicles to park. The building and parking area dropped off sharply in the back.

My parents never drank but my Uncle Charles did, and this was his haunt. Many fishing and hunting trips started and ended here. We kids usually took some pop and beer nuts to the car while the adults were inside. Sometimes fish and game were brought and shared with the patrons, some of whom practically lived there. Friday and Saturday nights saw an increase in visitors, and as the evening wore on and the drinking got more intense, fights would often erupt. Quickly escorted outside, the participants would continue fighting — sometimes even rolling down over the hill.

Drunken patrons would leave and often drive their cars off in the wrong direction. Depending on their speed, this would result in one of two outcomes: either their front wheels would be forced over the boards at the edge of the parking area, and their car would be left dangling in mid-air over the bank; or they'd go completely over the bank, into the field below. Either way, they were off the road.

All-in-all, The Polka Dot was just a typical beer joint — absolutely nothing fancy. While not being the only one around, it was my uncle's favorite. Most everything is gone today, but the notoriously steep hill still remains.

Moonshine, RWL, & Thunder Road

Hedgesville was not a dry town. The drink of choice varied as much as the cast of characters. There was no apparent reason why individuals chose certain drinks, but most were very loyal to their beverage.

Moonshiners were around but rarely seen by us kids. The Kate's Hollow area had a still or two, but they weren't very active. Some people, including my uncles, made grape or dandelion wine. I tried to make some with grapes and it was awful. The bugs hovering over it benefited the most.

"RWL" (short for run, walk, and lie down, so we thought) was perhaps the most popular beverage, given the number of bottles that could be found scattered along the roadside. Bottles would also accumulate at unofficial drinking spots, most of which were located along the creek near a bridge or swimming hole. Any "fishing" activities taking place at these locations were merely a disguise for an opportunity to drink. "Dipping suckers" meant pulling a net out of the water every hour or so and drinking all the time in between. Men firing kilns at the North Mountain Brick Plant often escaped down to Allensville Ford and drank there all night.

Thunder Road was a movie depicting moonshiners running alcohol on back roads with the law in hot pursuit. We also had this. Alcohol could be purchased cheaper in Maryland and brought into West Virginia without paying state taxes. It was then sold much more cheaply than at the state liquor stores that existed at that time. The vehicles used to do this trafficking were Plain Jane on the outside, but had very fast engines under the hoods. Years later I worked at a garage and got to see this first-hand.

Most towns had at least one town drunk. Even fictional Mayberry had its Otis. We had several. Some had regular jobs and only got drunk on the weekend. One in particular made drinking his life's work. I don't know how he afforded it, but he drank constantly and slept in his vehicle even in the dead of winter. Our drunks were friendly, or at least withdrawn, and didn't bother anyone. I now think they must have been very sad and lonely.

Our home was alcohol-free except for a beer or two — supposedly recommended by the doctor to aid in kidney function. My father never drank. How he avoided this I'll never know. He certainly was surrounded in town and at work with some real drinking characters.

Rolling Cigarettes

MY FATHER WAS A SMOKER — A CAMEL USER. No filters for him; they were packaged and ready to go. Some old-timers rolled their own. Under the metal can of tobacco was a drawer that held the papers. Some people carried tobacco in cloth pouches. They all had a particular ritual for creating the perfect cigarette.

The proper amount of tobacco would be placed on the paper and quickly rolled up. The paper was then licked lengthwise and rolled between the fingers. The ends were pinched and twisted shut. One gentleman had a rolling machine. When used properly, it produced smokes that looked like you had bought them.

As kids, we gave smoking a shot. Our parents told us not to smoke even though some of them did. I tried corn silk and the fruit of a cigar tree. We even made pipes from buckeyes. All were disgusting, and I found the whole idea of smoking to be awful. It hastened the death of my father at age 56 and ultimately killed both of my wife's parents.

As kids, we weren't aware of the dangers of smoking and just accepted the idea that most adults smoked. I have always viewed the need to smoke to be a need of people to find something to do with their hands. Rolling your own unfiltered cigarettes, I guess, increased the pleasure as well as hastened the death.

HALLOWEEN

HALLOWEEN WAS LOOKED FORWARD TO AS THE beginning of the cold-weather holiday season. A frosty night and the smell of burning leaves were part of the whole experience. Several times we even had a dusting of snow on the big night. In a town this small, no matter what your costume was, everybody knew your real identity. These were the days when trick-or-treating was done only within your own town. Today's practice of being driven by adults to another community or development didn't exist.

We began to plan our costumes a couple of days before Halloween. There seldom were any store-bought costumes or masks. With an old pair of bib overalls, a work coat, feed sacks, red handkerchiefs, old sheets, a stick, scissors, and a needle and thread, you went off to create — nothing exotic — but in a short time there appeared a hobo or a ghost. It didn't matter that it was the same costume as last year, because this was a new season.

There were no Halloween decorations for sale at the general store like the ones you find today. There were no strings of orange lights and plastic pumpkins. No orange trash bags with pumpkin faces, plastic ghosts in the trees, or houses with speakers outside playing eerie recordings could be found. At best, we had a pumpkin from which we carved a jack-o-lantern, and into which we placed a candle. It had a life expectancy of one or two days. Fresh pumpkin has its own unique smell, but burnt pumpkin is the worst.

After supper on Halloween night, we'd get ready. It did not matter how much advance preparation you had made, there was always a need for modification and adjustment. Sometimes nothing worked and you improvised. Ready or not, when it got dark, out you went, armed with as much of a bar of soap as you could find, and a trusty brown paper bag. Parents didn't worry because we roamed the town on a daily basis. You didn't have to look only for houses with their lights on. We'd visit the ones with their lights off, too.

The first stop was usually Poisal's Store. You'd walk in and stand beside the same glass case of penny candy that you saw each visit. Candy was selling for two or three pieces for a penny. We were given one or two pieces and sent on our way. Soap was used on the windows of anyone who didn't give you candy. This rule didn't apply to the store, however. Poisal's large glass windows provided the perfect surfaces for our soap-inscribed remarks — you just could not pass up the opportunity to write something on them.

After the store, you were off to haunt the town. We went from house to house in small groups. Meeting others, we'd stop and ask what they had gotten so as not to miss a home with potentially good stuff. We were looking for the biggest and best candy. Miniature or bite-size candy bars weren't really available then. Most people gave out the full-size bars, and we didn't want these gems to run out before our visit.

Some residents offered homemade goodies, including candy apples, cookies, and popcorn balls. There was no need to x-ray these treats. Our last stops were the homes offering sit-down snacks. We'd stand on their porches and yell, "Trick-or-Treat!" Someone would come to the door and overstate how cute or scary you were. You'd always hear, "I wonder who these children are?" as they escorted you to their kitchen table and fed you food and drinks — typically gingerbread and hot cider. The adults would talk continuously as we scarfed down the food. We were their entertainment and they weren't about to let us go without playing their version of 20 Questions. When we found a breach in their defenses, we made a quick escape, but only after thanking them. Politeness was important because the party lines would be busy the next day with conversation regarding the behavior of the children the night before.

When all possible goodies had been squeezed out of the town residents, we headed for home. My brother, sister, and I would dump our bags onto the floor, making sure our individual piles never touched. Now was the time for assessment. First, we compared the total volume and then the specific items. Being the oldest, I could roam farther, but the younger kids sometimes got more candy due to their cuteness or parental escorts. We were told not to eat too much — a measurement we considered vague, at best. The days to follow were spent enjoying the best candy first, as inventory rapidly reduced to undesirable varieties such as cinnamon-spiced hard candy. We'd oftentimes engage in trades — sometimes in *raids* — on each other's stash. Taking a small bite from your own favorite pieces of candy would ensure they would be spared from any looting.

This might be considered a dull time by today's standards. There weren't any lavish decorations or parties, and we did not destroy or vandalize property. Our only worries were guarding our stashes, and not feeling too sick by morning.

———

PAYING THE PHONE BILL

TODAY, WHEN YOU GET A PHONE BILL, YOU EITHER mail in a check, or pay online. That wasn't how it was done when I was a child. Calls were handled differently as well. We, like most others at the time, had a "party" line. It's crazy today to think that a system once existed where most "private" conversations were public. It was common to pick up the receiver and ask others to stop talking so you could use the phone. In later years we got a truly *private* line.

In Hedgesville, residents paid their telephone bills at the private home of two elderly sisters — Alice and Fanny Runk — who lived up the hill behind us. It was a duty that most of us would try to avoid. Nobody wanted to go there, not even the adults, as the sisters were starved for company. After knocking at the door, you were greeted by one of them and escorted across a cold, dark, cluttered room, through a doorway, and into their inner sanctum. This was the only room in their house that they occupied. It held a small kitchen, two beds, and a few uncomfortable pieces of furniture — all draped with fabric. In winter, the room would be extremely hot from a kerosene stove. The air was stagnant year-round, and always smelled of Vicks.

The problem with paying the phone bill was that once you were ushered into the home, you couldn't get out. You gave them the money, and then waited while they sat at a small cluttered table and prepared a receipt. People paying the phone bill must have been these old ladies' only link to the outside world, as they'd ask you about everything. They acted like relatives you visit once a year, saying how much you had grown, or how you resembled your parents. You would never sit down with the Runk sisters — Oh no! — that would've been the kiss of death. You just kept backing up toward the door to the next room, and to your freedom.

Once you attempted your escape through the doorway and into that cold, dark, cluttered room, you could sense the outside even if you couldn't quite see it yet. The sisters, usually draped in blankets or shawls, did not want to spend too much time in that room either, thank goodness. One of them would unlock the door, and before it was fully open, you would fly out, not even stopping to respond to whatever it was they were continuing to ask or tell you. It would be 30 days until your next phone bill ordeal.

I always tried to be scarce when our telephone bill was due, but as the oldest kid, I was usually the one who had to go pay it. Even my parents avoided this undesirable chore.

─∞∞∞─

THE FALLOUT SHELTER

I WAS LUCKY ENOUGH TO HAVE MY CHILDHOOD years fall between the end of World War II and the escalation of the war in Vietnam. Both of my mother's brothers — my Uncle Charles and Uncle Cronie — fought in World War II. Uncle Cronie — by the way — met Helen, the woman who would happen to become his future bride, at a hospital in her hometown of Bath, England, where he was convalescing after being wounded during battle. Neither of my uncles were quick to share their experiences of the war, but I was told enough to realize it was traumatic. Uncle Cronie shared only two stories that I can remember, and both were extremely disturbing, and amazingly heroic. Aunt Helen could not hear the sound of a thunderstorm without recalling the bombing, and experiencing a terrible panic. She would sit on her living room sofa, as stiff and still as she could, and silently wait for the storm to pass.

Prior to Vietnam, the Cold War had the most impact on my life. For years we anticipated a nuclear attack from Russia and, of course, retaliation from the United States. The Cuban Missile Crisis only heightened our concerns. Preparation for a nuclear attack occurred everywhere —

even in little Hedgesville. We saw films presenting tactics that would somehow protect us: ducking on your knees, covering your head, or hunkering under your desk, among others. School evacuation plans were formulated and the time it took for students to get home was calculated. The school was to be used as an emergency shelter and some supplies were stored there. It seemed, however, that getting us to our homes was the top priority. There was an inventory of items each household was advised to have, and of course, a secure location to remain until it was safe to rejoin the world, or whatever might be left of it. I have no idea of the number of Hedgesville families that were truly prepared for a nuclear disaster. Regardless, "home" was supposedly the safest place to survive an attack.

My family didn't really take the concept of emergency preparedness all that seriously. Our shelter would've been our basement, which realistically, we didn't exactly have. Our basement was more of a cellar. You opened the two, dilapidated wooden doors and went down several feet below the ground to a hand-dug space with a dirt floor. Columns of dry-fitted rocks supported the room above. You could clearly see daylight between the rocks. How much protection could an environment like this offer?

What might have been our future fallout shelter was stocked only with several jars of beans and tomatoes. Actually, it wasn't "stocked" at all. This was just where we stored our canned goods. There was usually a bin with potatoes — most of which were inedible. The food in the cellar might have kept us alive a few days, but there was no way to cook it. Regardless, we would not have perished immediately as an ample supply of water always ran in a channel across the floor. Last, but not least, we had no toilet facilities. Essentially, we had no emergency shelter.

There was one friend of mine, however, whose father had built a bona fide fallout shelter. It was below ground and constructed precisely to the established standards. You entered through a heavy door, walked several feet, turned left, walked a few more feet, and then found another door which opened into a large room.

This shelter was well-equipped with all of the food and supplies necessary to sustain life for quite some time. I was impressed the first time I saw it. It was obviously a well-considered shelter, unlike my family's cellar option. This particular shelter, though, had one commodity that was probably not on the list of officially required supplies — a stash of alcohol — perhaps the only inventory item that could provide an immediate, liquid-variety of comfort to adults who found themselves in the midst of a nuclear attack. We didn't consider this at the time, however. To us kids, this was a prime opportunity we just couldn't pass up. My friends and I only visited the shelter a handful of times, but each time we did, we got into the liquor. We would sample just a little, but soon enough, those "littles" left an obvious hole in the overall amounts. What to do?

We figured it out. We opened up the bottles and filled the voids with water. Who would know? Well, upon our next return to the shelter we learned who would know — anyone with eyes. Our refilling efforts had not been carried out with any exactness, and the uneven results were obvious.

We never returned to the shelter after this unfortunate discovery. I don't think any of our friends' parents ever knew we had been making visits there at the time, but probably realized so later, upon observing the collection of multi-leveled liquor bottles.

It's funny, but the nuclear threat didn't dominate our lives. We just accepted it and moved on. I guess this was normal. As a young teenager, there were more pressing concerns. So we kids did survive the Cold War — at times with a rather warm feeling in our stomachs.

—∞∞∞—

PICKING FRUIT

THERE WERE LOTS OF ORCHARDS AROUND HOME producing apples, peaches, and cherries. We even had some cherry trees in our own yard. They included sweet and sour red, along with a yellow wax. We ate them, and on rare occasions had enough extra to sell to our neighbors.

The orchards were a source of seasonal work for locals as well as groups of migrants who lived in camps provided by the orchard owners. If the orchard owner decided you were big, strong, and responsible enough, you could work several weeks here and there. Age was really not a factor — size was. I was over six feet tall before I became a teenager, so I passed that test. You also had to demonstrate that you could manage the heavy wooden ladders that were used at the time. If you passed this test, you were provided with a galvanized, two-gallon bucket and sent into the orchard.

I never tried thinning peaches, but spent a good deal of time in the cherry and apple orchards. Cherries became ripe in June and had a short season, lasting only several weeks. Porterfield's Orchard was a few miles from home, so an adult would drive some of us kids there to work, and pick us up later in the evening.

The foreman directed you to each tree that you were to pick. Picking from the ground was easy and you could use both hands to rake the cherries into a bucket. Midway up the tree, on a ladder resting against a branch, you picked a little slower, but it was still profitable.

Topping the tree was the worst task of all. The cherries were far apart and it was necessary to position the ladder many different times to pick all the fruit. Not allowed — but often done — was the technique of pounding your ladder against the limb and knocking the cherries to the ground. The objective was to move as quickly as possible to the next tree and to more cherries. When you thought the tree had been well-cleared, you called for the foreman who rendered his decision. He could make you climb up to get two or three more cherries hanging on a limb, or scold you if he saw too many cherries scattered on the ground. If you were caught pounding the tree, you were fired.

Picking cherries was a hot, sticky job. After only a few minutes, you were covered in sweat and cherry juice, which would spray your face and burn your eyes, and run down your arms and soak your shirt. By the day's end, your arms would stick to your sides. I tried picking cherries both with, and without, a shirt. There was no significant difference.

After each bucket was full of cherries, you took it to a collection point where it was inspected. If accepted, it was dumped into a large container. They maintained a record of the number of buckets you picked. We also kept our own mental tallies. I believe the going rate was 20¢ per bucket for your first 20 buckets. The rate for any buckets beyond 20 increased to 25¢ per bucket.

Most days it was difficult to exceed the 20-bucket mark, but sometimes you got good trees that were loaded and could really make those cherries fly. The season was short and we were paid when it was over. We received a check from $30 to $40 for two weeks of work. I thought I was rich. I remember setting aside $17 to go to Boy Scout camp and keeping $5 for crafts and snacks. Our town had a firemen's festival to raise money for our fire department, and I saved several dollars to spend there. A few dollars were kept in reserve for emergencies.

Apples came on in the fall. Groups of migrants, mainly from Jamaica, traveled between orchards, picking the fruit. I was amazed how fast the migrant workers could empty the trees! Being late in the fall, there was only a short time on weekday evenings that we kids could work, as we were already back in school. We could, however, work all day on

Saturdays. I would bicycle to and from the apple orchard and sometimes get home well after dark on Saturday nights. Picking apples required climbing the very same ladders used for picking cherries, but we now had picking baskets which were designed to wear over the shoulders. They were constructed of canvas with a metal, half-moon rim to form an opening. When full to capacity, they were quite heavy and pulled you forward as you'd empty it repeatedly into your bushel box. Each picker had a specific number, and when your bushel box was full, you placed into it a paper tag with your number on it. This was an honest operation, and nobody ever thought of cheating.

After all the trees were picked, we moved on to ground apples — the ones that had fallen and were used for juice. The migrants didn't bother with this slow task as it wasn't really profitable. We kids, not fully realizing the time/value ratio, would get down on hands and knees, crawl around the trees, and pick ground apples. Some apples were solid, but many were soft and had already begun to rot. Some were occasionally filled with bees. The temperature was cold and the apples would freeze to the ground. Digging them out wasn't fun. Gloves got in the way so exposed fingers did the job.

Ellis's Orchard used 22-bushel boxes for collecting their apples, and it seemed like forever until you got them filled. Someone at the orchard used a tractor to move the boxes on ahead of you, anticipating the tree at which you would get your box completely filled. I don't remember the pay scale, but needless to say, we didn't get rich.

Sometimes at Porterfield's Orchard, I was paid by the hour to load trucks at the packing shed, where the apples were sorted, cleaned, graded, packed into boxes, and then loaded onto a tractor trailer truck. Box after box came rolling down the metal conveyor belt, and were stacked to the roof of the trailer. It might have been cool outside, but there was no air circulating inside the trailer, and it became very hot. This was *not* my favorite job.

Many of these old orchards remain, but some are not maintained, and others became housing developments. I hope some of the orchards will always be there. As I drive between Hedgesville and Martinsburg in the spring, the fruit trees are pink and white with blossoms. The smell of their flowers and the first tint of color means spring is here. In the fall, the placement of boxes along the road means harvest is near. This usually triggers a memory of crawling on my knees and prying frosty apples from the ground.

MOVIES

MARTINSBURG, AT ONE TIME, HAD SEVERAL downtown movie theaters. Once in a while my father took me to the Apollo or the Central. This was a real treat. We would sometimes go to the Blue White Grill and get several burgers or hot dogs and take them with us to the theater. My father liked to sit up in the balcony on one side of the theater. There were two seats next to each other, with one being elevated a foot or so above the other.

I don't remember many of the movies, but most were science fiction. He took me to see *Rodan*. I got so scared that I visited the rest room to avoid seeing some of it. Once, when my father and I returned home after one such movie, my mother, who never went, made a comment that the mantle in the living room looked like it could walk. In my sci-fi state of mind, I became even more scared thinking something supernatural was going to happen right in our house. She only meant it was cluttered and looked awful.

When allowed to go to movies by myself, I would head to the Strand Theatre on Saturday afternoon where I was joined by dozens of other kids my age. There were usually two or three movies, and they were always horror flicks starring a vampire or giant creature. The movies cost little to attend, and you usually got a gift such as vampire teeth. You couldn't hear much of the movie over the chatter. Kids were mostly there so their parents could be someplace else. The real gimmick was that if you stayed for all the movies, you earned a pass to get in free the following Saturday.

All of the old movie theaters in town are now gone, but the Apollo still remains as a civic theater and hosts plays and musicals. I'm always reminded of going to the movies when I flip through the TV channels and find a Japanese monster flick where a creature hatches out of a giant egg and crashes into the cardboard buildings.

French's Viewing

THIS IS A BRIEF STORY, BUT THE EXPERIENCE LEFT a lasting impression in my mind. The French family was living beside my grandmother when Mr. French died. My cousins and I were very young. We were led into their house and ushered to the living room. The room was quite small and everyone was huddled around the casket which contained Mr. French. This was probably our first up-close-and-personal encounter with a dead person.

I can't remember what words were spoken, or how long we were there. I have never been to another viewing held at someone's private residence, as it is no longer a local practice. It's funny how things stick with you. My Aunt Helen later lived in the house beside the French's, and I'd always remember that experience when I visited her. I can still picture the dead person in the living room.

———

THE CLAYTONS

M R. AND MRS. CLAYTON WERE A BLACK COUPLE who lived on Route 9, down from the town spring. The Claytons had employment in Washington, D.C., and I remember them as being rather sophisticated residents of our town. They were well-dressed, drove a nice car, and owned several houses. The Claytons were, in fact, my grandparents' neighbors, as well as their landlords. They were generous and kind, and would offer their extra garden space to my family to plant. To us kids, the Claytons had it all, but we quickly became aware of the impermanent nature of life when we witnessed a tragedy unfold one day.

The location of this event was in the graveyard behind the Episcopal Church. This graveyard extended down the hill in the direction of the elementary school. We walked through it on a regular basis when we would head to the schoolyard to play ball. The cemetery's gravel road was narrow and had many looping turns. You traveled it almost at a crawl. On this particular day, while playing ball, we heard the sound of an engine revving up and gravel being thrown. We looked up to witness the Clayton's car crashing head-on into a very large, cemetery tree. We immediately ran to the scene, but quickly jumped back when we caught sight of the aftermath of the accident.

We later learned that Mr. Clayton had suffered a heart attack when he was driving through the cemetery. When this happened, his foot pressed down on the accelerator, causing the car to speed right into a tree. Upon impact, Mrs. Clayton was thrown forward in the passenger seat. This car was fancy and had seat belts, which most of us had never before seen. The force of the accident was such that the belt had cut into her waist, opening a gash which resulted in severe blood loss. She died shortly thereafter.

This was not a pleasant event to witness then, or to write about now. My mother's parents and brothers are buried in that cemetery, and I think of the accident when I visit. The tree is gone, but not the memory.

—∞∞∞—

DEAD MAN ON A SHOVEL

WHEN THE ALARM AT THE TOWN FIRE HALL sounded, everybody in the area would stop and take note. A few minutes would pass as we waited to hear the siren stop, indicating the call had been answered. We'd watch to see the direction in which the truck was heading. Listening to the truck siren would also tell you if the truck was traveling out of town or staying local.

On one occasion in particular, I remember following the truck on my bike as it headed up the street and out on Cannon Hill Road. I knew it couldn't be going too far as the houses ended about a mile out that road. There was a cluster of about five or six houses situated across from an old schoolhouse. When I arrived at the location where the truck was, I saw a house was burning, shooting flames into the air. The house was directly across from another home where we used to go to pick berries.

Someone came out of the house and walked toward a large tree. He was carrying a big coal shovel, which he placed near the base of the tree. He used a burlap bag to cover up both the shovel and its contents. We could tell that whatever was on the shovel had been on fire as it was still smoldering. Curiosity got the best of a few of us onlookers, so someone lifted one of the corners of the bag. Under the burlap was the smoldering remains of what had recently been a living person. This man had obviously been in the house when it caught on fire, and failed to make it out in time. The sack was immediately replaced and we scattered fast. The smell was awful, and was probably worse than the site of the contorted, smoldering body.

In our lives there are events that secure a spot in our minds and are terribly difficult — if not impossible — to forget. This is one of those such events. It did not cause lasting problems, but did leave a lasting memory. I have been witness to several deaths — most of which have been in sterile and expected environments. I have seen some train and car accidents with horrible consequences that have left images I will never forget. But that terrible fire scene — with its sights and smells — made a permanent home in my head.

PART THREE

FUN AND GAMES

GAMES

ONCE IN A WHILE, WHEN I CALL MY GRANDKIDS, I'll ask them what they're up to. They often reply, "Nothing" and then complain of being bored. Perhaps they mean that the things they *can* do just aren't that exciting. It's hard for me to fully grasp "childhood boredom."

Boredom was never an issue when I was a kid, nor was finding something to do. Rather, our problem was usually a shortage of time in which to do these things. Games varied depending on the weather. On the days we couldn't play outside, we'd play board games, including Checkers, Sorry, Uncle Wiggly, and Monopoly. We also played card games, including rummy, hearts, canasta, and sometimes bridge.

We took turns invading each others' homes and taking advantage of their selections. The Fierys had a Carrom board and Snooks taught us how to play. The Hites had indoor versions of our favorite outdoor games, including an electric football game, along with a baseball and basketball game. The football game used plastic figures and their movement down the field was caused by the vibration created when the game was switched on. The baseball game had a small wooden bat attached to it that was used to hit small magnetic balls against a metal base. Ping-pong balls were used in the basketball game. These indoor games were okay, but we preferred to play outside.

Outdoor games ran the gamut and some required absolutely no equipment. We played softball, baseball, whiffle ball, basketball, and football. Whiffle ball suited just about any yard, and required only two people — a pitcher and a batter. We played in several yards around town, and each "stadium" had its own set of rules. Hitting the ball past the outhouse was a double; hitting the house above the kitchen window, or over the church hedge, was a home run. We knew the rules for each particular field.

We once got the urge to play golf. The only problem was that we had no real golfing equipment, nor a golf course.

No problem. We were resourceful children and took pride in our improvisational skills. We dug holes in the ground and used softballs as golf balls, and bats for clubs. On another day, we wanted to play horse shoes, but since we couldn't afford a play set, we simply used real horse shoes. They didn't work too well, so the Riser family and ours went together and bought a real set. We played the color right off of the shoes. We pitched in the garden and along the alley beside the Riser's. The clanging must have driven all our parents crazy. We kept playing as long as we were challenged, and until our fingers bled and formed hard calluses. If the score was 3 to 1 we would yell, "Oil!" If the score became 18 to 14, we broke into a verse of "The Battle of New Orleans." Get it?

Games requiring minimal or no equipment included Hide-and-Seek, Kick-the-Can, and our personal favorite, Hunt-the-Grey-Fox. This expanded version of Hide-and-Seek allowed — even encouraged — players to hide as far from home base as possible. "Far" could often mean a half mile, and this expanded playing field created a challenge for both teams. If you were "it," you were to find everyone else who was hiding. If you couldn't find anyone you would yell, "Lost trail!" Those hiding were to respond, "Hunt the grey fox!" You can imagine that if you were *it*, you were *it* for the entire evening, and that lasted well into the night.

The truth of the matter is that many of the people doing the hiding would do so only briefly, and then go home to bed. Sometimes the hunter would do the same. You never quite knew when the game was over, so at some point, you just gave up and went looking for some action. We never discussed this phenomenon at the time, but always thought the honor system had a few flaws.

Pitching Pennies

IF YOU HAVE NEVER TRIED THIS SPORT, YOU HAVE missed out on a marvelous waste of time. The idea is to carefully toss a penny in the direction of a line — usually the groove between sections of sidewalk.

We had a barber shop and adjoining dentist office, both sharing a tin roof that covered the sidewalk. The concrete underneath was protected from the elements, and was smooth, with perfectly straight cracks. What a wonderful place to pitch pennies on rainy days! The task was to toss a penny toward the line from a predetermined distance. Landing on the line was your goal. The closest penny to the line, won. Another variation was to use a wall as the target, but we all preferred the sidewalk crack option.

No one ever got rich from this, as the money just seemed to be redistributed among the players. We probably never had more than 10¢ each to begin with, and I can not recall anyone going broke. This was the time of "wheat" pennies and the less common, but always available, 1943 steel penny. We would get them in the change at Poisal's Store. Some players loved the '43 steel pennies, and others would never use them. I actually preferred them. Their sound was distinct, and they hugged the concrete better.

As I said, this was a mindless activity. Several players would toss, and then everyone would walk to the line and argue over who was closest. Sometimes it required the use of sophisticated equipment such as a twig to measure proximity and confirm an official winner.

Under that tin roof, against the background of the gray barber shop and unpainted dentist office, the light was reduced. Add to this a cloudy sky and you have a dreary, gray-green environment. This was our penny pitching arena. The arena is long gone, but the sound of rain on the tin roof and pennies hitting the concrete can still conjure up a memory of our sport.

BROWN'S MULE
CHEWING TOBACCO

L ONG BEFORE THE SURGEON GENERAL WARNED about tobacco use, my parents told me not to use any tobacco products. My father, however, did *not* follow his own advice and smoked heavily. We were surrounded by smokers and chewers. This wasn't just the realm of men, as some women smoked and dipped snuff as well.

Our parents' warnings did not seem to prevent us kids from experimenting with tobacco, and I can assure you — it was more fun to be on the giving end, rather than the receiving end, of our tobacco antics. For a nickel, we would buy a plug of Brown's Mule. It was a coarse, hard block of tobacco about the size of a pack of cigarettes. We'd gang up on someone, hold him down, and pry his mouth open. We'd then force the plug, or a large part of it, into our victim's mouth, holding it shut for several minutes. During this time the plug softened, and the victim's mouth became full of black, juicy spit.

You knew it was working when he began to gag and juice ran out of his mouth. You then pinched his nose shut, allowing his mouth to open slightly, and waited for our victim to swallow. Then, seeing him becoming really sick, we would let go and run — far enough away to escape, but close enough to watch everything. We'd stop and laugh, but always remember how it felt, as most of us had also been victims at one time. What a sick prank if you were on the receiving end, but what sick fun to watch if you weren't.

TOMATO, HEDGE APPLE, AND CRAB APPLE BATTLES

EACH YEAR IN THE FALL, GARDENS IN TOWN HAD an ample supply of unripened tomatoes. At the end of the alley, behind our barn, was an old hedge apple tree which produced plenty of its knobby, brain-like, grapefruit-sized fruit. A crab apple tree grew in the lower corner of our yard, and the fruit was rarely harvested. This produce had no practical use, except to us kids.

Tomatoes, hedge apples, and crab apples were superb ammunition for our battles. There were no rules or chosen teams. We'd gather as much of our organic ammunition as we could and then search for a hiding place, usually around the corner of a building. Anyone who ventured close enough was attacked and usually ran in retreat, with the attacker in hot pursuit. Stopping to turn around and reason with your enemy was useless. You just hoped they would run out of ammunition so you could pummel them.

Little mercy was shown toward your enemy. Smashing fruit on top of their head was acceptable. Tomatoes could sting, and a hedge apple, delivered with force, could knock you down. There was no mutually-agreed-upon stopping point, and our games either fizzled out or ended in one gigantic fight. On one occasion, while running through the garden to escape attack, I fell and impaled my lip on a freshly cut corn stalk sticking just a few inches up from the ground. It was a real treat to pull my lip off of the stalk — much like John Wayne yanking an arrow from his leg. This injury required a trip to the hospital for several stitches. With a towel over my eyes and little anesthetic, they sewed me up while I formulated my plan for revenge.

Snow and Sledding

NOTHING IN WINTERTIME WAS MORE EAGERLY anticipated than snow. When you must create your own entertainment, what could be better than a totally transfigured landscape and endless opportunities for fun?

Snowfalls seemed deeper and days seemed colder then. Many times, a hard crust several inches thick made it possible to walk on top of the snowdrifts. However, as I write this in mid-February, it's the second day of a snow storm with an expected accumulation of 36 inches. The air temperature is now 12°F and the wind chill is -1°F. Shortly before her death, my mother told my wife and me that the first snow of each season would be her gift to us. Boy, are we getting gifts this year!

Living on a hilltop with other hills all around us, sled riding was a great sport. We had several sleds, including a Lightning Glider, which were kept in the loft above the barn. When snow arrived, out they came, complete with rusty runners and exposed nails. Sandpaper and a hammer made the repairs quick and easy to complete. Actually, our biggest challenge was finding the appropriate clothing and getting the layers on. Black rubber boots with metal clasps and at least two pairs of pants were put on first. This was followed by several shirts, a sweater, and your "play" coat, which used to be your "good" coat until you outgrew it. It became even tighter with so much clothing on underneath. Finally, on went the hat and gloves. With our movement restricted, and walking much like Frankenstein's monster, out we went. What you must understand is that only the boots were waterproof. Within a very short time you were covered with snow and getting wetter by the minute.

With a frozen piece of rope attached to the front of the sled, we headed to a hill. The road in front of Donaldson's house was not the longest hill but was a primary location for sledding. Mason's hill was longer, steeper, and more exciting. Vehicle traffic would pack the snow down, making it icy. The only problem with both of these hills was that you could go too fast and end up out on the state highway. Using Mason's hill, you had several roads branching off to potentially avoid the highway. There was very little traffic, and everyone would yell, "Car!" if one turned onto the hill.

We would sled for hours. We'd belly flop, sit and push off, do a double-decker, or form a train. We installed jumps, most of which failed to work. In addition to sleds, we would go down the hills on lids from ringer washing machines, coal shovels, or even car hoods. If we happened to be at the bottom of the hill when a car came along, we'd "hop the car" back up. This meant grabbing the bumper, falling onto your sled, and being pulled, often undetected by the driver. We were told stories of people hopping cars for miles, even to Martinsburg — possibly true, but incredibly dangerous.

If the car stopped abruptly, you could be slammed into the bumper, or even pushed under the car.

We liked variety and change, and thinking more fun could be had elsewhere, we ventured around town. Potato Hill was the longest run in town but also had the longest walk back to the top. Open fields were everywhere. Brown's field was exciting because of its frozen pond in the center. The frozen water level was a foot or so below the adjoining ground, so we'd make a ramp from the pond to the snow to complete the run. Across the pond and up the ramp you'd fly, shooting out over a bank several feet above the ground before landing back in the snow and coming to a stop. I missed the ramp once, and hit the bank at high speed, embedding my sled. My body, however, stayed in motion. Exposed sled nails ripped the buttons off my coat, and I rolled over the edge of the pond and into the field below. We had no major accidents, just lots of cuts and bruises. Nobody cared, as we were numb from the cold. What you can't feel doesn't count when you're a kid.

In between sledding, we had time for snowball fights. These battles were waged from behind forts constructed of cylindrical snow blocks molded from galvanized buckets. The blocks were neatly stacked on top of each other and cemented together with packed snow. When snows were especially deep, we made igloos, placing a rug on the floor and using candles for light. These activities were fun, but sledding was always our favorite.

We sometimes would build a bonfire to keep us warm, but eventually we had to call it quits. With red faces and frozen dripping noses, we marched home, usually covered in frozen, matted snow, looking like West Virginia "yetties." Clothes were stripped off and placed on the newspapers that Mom had arranged on the kitchen floor. We would leave our last layer on and go huddle above the floor register in the living room, thawing out to the sound of snow chunks falling onto the metal grate below. As the feeling returned to our extremities, we remembered our snowy triumphs and imagined our next day's adventures.

When my children were young, we went sledding on a small hill in front of our home and sometimes we went to fields. I still do this with my grandchildren, only now we use plastic toboggans, over-inflated inner tubes, and snow boards. We'll sled some tomorrow, only my wife tells me the projected snowfall has been increased to more than 36 inches over the next two days. I expect I'll spend more time moving snow than sledding on it.

—⟨∞⟩—

SOAP BOX RACER

OUR TOYS WITH WHEELS CONSISTED OF ROLLER skates, bicycles, and an old horse-drawn buggy — without the horse. We skated where there were sidewalks, and rode around town on bikes. The buggy was large, and we'd push each other through the garden until its narrow wheels would get stuck in the loose dirt.

At an auction at the Nadenbousch house I spotted a real soap box racer. Marvin and his father had built it from a kit and painted it West Virginia blue and gold, of course. My father reluctantly bought it, complete with helmet, for $10, and we pushed it home. Its brake was a shoe heel that would drag on the ground and supposedly stop the vehicle.

My father told us to keep it in the yard. We had a large yard and pushed ourselves around the grassy parts. This wasn't much fun. With all of the available paved roads with hills, it seemed like such a waste to keep it in the yard.

Knowing better, but unable to stop ourselves, we set off for the hill in front of the Methodist church. My friends and I seemed sure that, by placing some kids just above the intersection of this road and Route 9, the racer could be stopped before entering the crossroads.

Nobody volunteered to be the first to go down the hill. We somehow talked Eddie, the preacher's son, into being the pilot. I pushed him off at the top of the hill while my cousins waited at the intersection below. The racer was well constructed, had good wheels, and went fast. I stood with an open mouth as the racer kept picking up speed and shot past my cousins, across the state highway, past Poisal's, and up the hill to the high school, where it finally came to a stop. All the residents along its path saw the blue and gold flash streak by. We ran to Eddie, retrieved the racer, and pushed it home and back into our yard. It was a small town and something like this wouldn't be kept a secret for long.

I knew the secret was out when my father arrived home from work. His route home was the same path the racer had traveled, only reversed. Indeed, our racer was gone next day, sold to the Moore family. It had been ours only three days, and in that time, we almost killed Eddie. Thank God the traffic on Route 9 was light then. The odds of him crossing that road today, without being hit, are slim.

Martinsburg resumed the Soap Box Derby several years ago. I read articles about it in the paper and can't help but think of my brief time owning the racer. Go get 'em Eddie! You were the Blue-and-Gold Streaker of Hedgesville.

—◦◦◦—

HOMEMADE MOTORCYCLE

I HAD A BIG, RED-AND-BLACK ROADMASTER BICYCLE with no gears or hand brakes. I rode my bike everywhere, and logged many miles — mostly for fun, but sometimes to work at the orchards. To make our bikes sound impressive, we would attach pieces of cardboard or balloons to the fenders, producing a motor-like sound as they brushed against the spokes of the turning wheels. Clothespins were used to attach the cardboard. Balloons were tied on.

My father once helped me try to put a real motor on my bike. We took the engine from a lawn mower and mounted it on a platform which we built over the rear fender. With the use of belts, levers, and much jerry-rigging, you pushed down a long metal rod, engaged the motor, and sort of took off. There was no real clutch.

Two big problems were the bike's weight, and stopping it. The motor weighed so much and sat up so high that you could barely balance the bike. Taking off normally was impossible. Someone had to steady the bike and push you to get things moving. As you gathered speed you could engage the motor. Tipping over, especially when making a turn, was a real problem.

Next came the important issue of stopping. On a normal bike, you just stopped peddling and applied the coaster brakes. To stop this thing, you needed nine hands. You had to push a throttle back to idle, pull a lever back to release the belt from the engine, and apply the coaster brakes — all while trying not to fall over from all the weight.

We soon realized this was a bad idea and put the motor back on the mower. It was easier to pedal than try to handle our awkward creation. It was, however, fun to try.

⤛⦿⤜

INNER-TUBE
AND BLIND-SPRING GUNS

THERE WAS ALWAYS A FASCINATION ABOUT GUNS as a boy. Maybe this was because real guns were everywhere, but kept just out of our reach. We looked forward to getting our first real guns, but also enjoyed the stop-gap weapons we were able to create.

There was a weapon that just about anyone could make: the inner-tube gun. All you needed was a clothespin, two pieces of wood, and an old inner tube. One piece of wood 12 to 18 inches long served as the barrel, and was nailed to another piece of wood about four to six inches long, which created the handle. A clothespin was nailed to the handle, and a V-shaped notch was cut at the end of the barrel. The inner tube was cut into circular segments about a half-inch wide — glorified rubber bands, essentially.

You operated the gun by placing a band in the notch at the end of the barrel, stretching it back, and clipping it in place with the clothespin. There was a limit to the stretching, though, because the grip of a clothespin can only hold a certain tension. When the gun fired, the band would go forward with both minimal accuracy, and minimal force. The longer the barrel, the greater the force. You could make inner tube guns from scraps and shoot them at your friends with little danger of causing injury.

When it came to distance and ease of construction, the blind-spring gun was — hands down — your best option. You needed only an old window blind and a saw. You would remove all the blind material, leaving just the wooden tube housing the spring, which also happened to be the built-in ammunition. You would very carefully remove a metal cap from one end of the tube — and I mean carefully — as the spring inside would shoot out. The tube could be sawed off a foot or so back from the end, thus allowing maximum compression for greater force.

The gun was fired by compressing and releasing the spring after attempting to aim. It had tremendous force and traveled many yards, but with no accuracy. We tried to shoot birds that were sitting on the ground. Rest assured, no birds ever stood a chance of being harmed.

BB Rifles

OUR PRE-GUNPOWDER WEAPON OF CHOICE WAS the BB rifle. Mine was a Daisy pump, and like in the movie *A Christmas Story*, we heard "You'll shoot your eye out!" and were warned not to shoot at birds and windows. Eyes were lucky, but birds and windows — not so much.

We bought our BBs for 10¢ a tube at Poisal's Store, and a tube could last several days. BBs were great for shooting pigeons in barns, as they'd shoot the bird without hurting the roof. We sometimes shot at stationary targets, but preferred things which moved. Perhaps the dumbest thing ever attempted was taping a .22-caliber rifle shell to the end of the barrel and firing the BB rifle. The bullet would fire on occasion, and when it did, it just went wherever it wanted. We were lucky that nobody was seriously injured. Kids, please don't attempt any variation of this at home.

MATTEL PISTOLS

DAVEY CROCKETT WAS ALL THE RAGE IN 1956. That Christmas, Santa Claus brought my brother and me buckskin outfits of sorts, and real Mattel pistols! The pistols were excellent — six-shooters with holsters and a belt to hold extra cartridges. You'd load the gun by forcing a gray plastic projectile into a metal cartridge which housed a spring. When you fired the gun, the plastic projectile shot several feet, at best. It couldn't hurt a fly and accuracy was poor. Mattel pistols only proved effective at shooting, but never toppling, folded pieces of paper that we lined up across the front of the sofa. We would lie on the floor and shoot and shoot, and sometimes even hit our targets.

PING-PONG BALL GUN

A PING-PONG BALL GUN WAS HARMLESS, BUT MORE powerful than a Mattel pistol. It held a few balls. You slid the lever under the barrel to build up pressure. When fired, the ball traveled a distance, but the impact had almost no force. It was sort of accurate and could sting up-close. We had only one, and when it broke, there were no more.

COLLECTING COINS

I DON'T KNOW HOW IT STARTED, BUT A GROUP OF US kids got some blue coin books at the Five and Dime and our collecting began. Soon we were self-declared experts at the hobby. I had a small amount of money in my stash, and my parents let me check their change. Slowly the coins were located and pushed into their appropriate spots in the coin book. Pennies, nickels, and dimes were my limit. The best part was that our general store would sell us a roll of pennies. I would take the roll home and search through it. If you found any usable ones, you took them out and put the rejects back in the roll, returned it to the store and exchanged it for another. Several of us kids were doing this, so the clerks probably got tired of seeing us, but if they did, they never really let on.

We soon learned which coins were the most valuable and we searched hard to find them. I don't know what made us think we would find them in our little town, but we kept searching anyway. We discovered a little history along the way as to who had designed what coin and the year of its release. We became well-versed in the rarity, quality, and condition of coins. We learned why pennies were once made from steel, and why Buffalo nickels were so difficult to date.

It didn't take long to see that there were more holes in our coin books than we could possible fill from the town store. I responded to a Littleton Coin Company ad in the back of my *Boys' Life* magazine. They sent a catalog with their prices and an order form. We used their price list to quickly calculate the value of our own collections. All of our coins were in "Very Fine" condition, of course, even if you could barely see the date. We were getting wealthier by the minute, at least according to our estimates.

On several occasions, I ordered some hard-to-find coins by mail. It was quite an event when the envelope with my name on the front arrived in our mailbox. Inside was a catalog, along with the small brown envelopes containing my purchases. I examined the coins and placed them into my collection book. Somehow I always expected that the book would look much more full after I added the coins.

I completed several books over the years and eventually my children will inherit the collection. Even though I now have no interest in the hobby, I do try to find the new state quarters and keep a set for each grandchild. Perhaps all the kids will think their collections are as valuable as I once did.

I do hope they will realize, however, the hours I invested in searching for coins — a process, which for the great kid coin collectors of Hedgesville, was the most fun part of all.

———

COUNTING CARS

T HE INTERSECTION OF STATE ROUTES 9 AND 901 marked the center of town. One of each of the corners was home to the following: a pool hall, a portion of Poisal's Store, a house with large buckeye trees, and a closed store with a large concrete stoop next to the sidewalk.

This was our staging site for events and also served as a place to loaf, watch the world go by, and count cars. In the 1950s, traffic on Route 9, which was the main highway connecting us to Martinsburg, wasn't anything like it is today. You could sit for quite some time before seeing a car pass by. Today there is a continuous flow.

We would pick a particular make of vehicle and see how many of its models would pass by in a certain amount of time. This also included tractor trailers, as there were no interstate highways. Nobody cared who won. This was just something to do until someone suggested a new adventure and off we would go.

─◈◈◈─

SKILLS:
ACCOMPLISHMENTS & TATTOOS

L OAFING WAS NEVER A WASTE OF TIME. WE OFTEN found ourselves sitting on porch steps or hanging out on the corner, sharing our latest skills or accomplishments.

Talents varied greatly along with the degree of difficulty they carried. I'm not talking about athletic or intellectual skills, but rather raw human abilities. These self-taught skills had a brief life expectancy, were readily shared, but were rarely exhibited to adults.

Making disgusting sounds cost no money and would always get a laugh. Belching was one such sound. Gulping air or drinking a lot of pop always preceded the feat. We created contests for length and volume. One boy was the town champion of both. He could loudly belch the entire alphabet. How can you beat that?

Noises from another body part were equally popular, and socially unacceptable. It was always more impressive to produce the actual sound. If this wasn't possible, there was a substitute. Placing one hand in your armpit and pulling the other down quickly could produce a comparable sound, but lacked the crowd-scattering capability of the real deal.

Some of our skills required accessories, and tattooing was one of them. We acquired tattoos as prizes in bubble gum wrappers and in Cracker Jack boxes. Applying them correctly was an art. Since money was scarce, it seemed a waste to use a temporary tattoo for only one impression on one person. We prided ourselves in multiple inkings.

Hands and forearms were popular locations. We rubbed them clean with spit — an important, and readily available commodity. The tattoo master waited until you had applied the correct amount of spit to the designated area. He then carefully placed the paper containing the transfer on the area and gently rubbed it. At the correct time, he lifted one corner and removed the paper. If done correctly, you had a perfect tattoo. While still wet, the paper was taken to the next person in line, placing it on their spit-covered skin. More pressure was required for the second impression, as there was less ink. We tried to ink as many people as possible with one tattoo, but with diminishing returns.

Sporting your new markings, you had a good excuse not to go near water. At the moment of their creation, they were considered museum-quality works of art. As a child, nothing appeared permanent, and this remained true for our inkings, along with other more crude habits.

MALLOW CUPS

THIS CHOCOLATE-AND-COCONUT-CRÈME–FILLED delight cost you a nickel. A Mallow Cup was, however, twice the fun. The cardboard square at the bottom of the wrapper was printed with a large number, representing a value ranging from 5¢ to $1. Your goal was to collect these cards and reach a value of $5. When you reached this total, you mailed the cards away and in return, received a box of 10 candy bars. You'd eat them quickly, hoping to collect $5 worth of cards again. How neat this was! Eating lots of candy bars helped you earn more free ones later. Mallow Cups are still around, but now it takes 500 points and the cost of a postage stamp to receive a lousy $1 rebate check.

ROLLER SKATING

ONLY A FEW KIDS IN TOWN ROLLER SKATED. We had some concrete sidewalks, but there were no large paved areas upon which to skate. Adjustable metal clamp-on skates were all we owned, and each of us had our own skate key. Continual adjustments were necessary, as finding the correct amount of pressure to apply against our rubber-soled shoes was a fine art. There were no knee pads or helmets — just lots of scratches and bruises.

I was luckier than most kids, as my father really enjoyed roller skating. He was not only a skater, but also a very good skater. There were a couple of rinks within an hour's drive and we went to them several times each year. My father had even worked at a few of them when he was younger, including Hillside and Ridgeway Rinks in West Virginia, and Berryville Rink in Virginia. Berryville Rink is where my father and mother first met. Hillside Rink is where I learned how to roller skate. The corners there were faced-off with boards, creating triangles. These triangular areas were protected from the other skaters, and were perfect places for beginners to practice and learn.

My father never danced, nor showed much interest in music at home, but when it came to skating, that was a different story. He had his own skates, which were black with red toe stops. He was a natural, and after stepping into the rink, he appeared to simply float across the hardwood floor. He put his hands in his pockets and became one with the music. Whether skating forward or backward — the envy of those who could barely stand in skates — he made it look effortless.

Roller rinks of the 1950s and '60s were nothing like the ones my grandchildren skate in today. Most were narrow and not very long. I was told that some had been converted from World War II-era chicken houses. They looked like chicken houses. There were no strobe lights or fancy laser displays, and certainly no air conditioning. They did have a large mirrored ball hanging in the center of the rink to provide the only mood lighting.

Our closest rink was Hillside, also called Hillside Lake Park. Its name described its location, not its setting. It was built on a rather steep hill, touching the ground on one side and being supported by poles on the other. It had many windows running along the two long walls. If you stopped to look out a window on the pole side, it was a rather long drop to the ground. Hillside Rink was hot in the summer, and cold in the winter.

You could rent either shoe skates, or the less-expensive, clamp-on variety. Shoe skates were a luxury, but I got them often, possibly because the people behind the counter gave my dad a discount when they remembered that he used to work there. We circled the rink to organ music which played over large, ceiling-mounted speakers. Things would be changed up once in a while with a couples-only skate, or the surprisingly awkward reverse-direction skate. If you really wanted to impress onlookers, you could demonstrate your more advanced technical skills to a novelty song such as the "Hokey Pokey."

We would skate and sweat for hours on end. There was no birthday party area or fancy concession stand. We just sat on wooden benches behind a wooden rail, and enjoyed bottled soda and packaged snacks that were offered for refreshments. I can't remember how much anything cost, but it wasn't much. For a time they even had a bus that would transport people from the square in Martinsburg to the rink in Hillside. This didn't help since I lived out in Hedgesville. These old familiar rinks are now gone. Hillside ended up becoming a bar, and later burned down.

Martinsburg now has a fancy new rink, complete with laser displays, party area, expanded food selections, and of course, air conditioning and heat. This new facility is certainly more accommodating and comfortable than the rinks I grew up with, but I don't know if it is any more enjoyable. Skating rinks were always exciting adventures for the whole family, and provided us all the perfect environment to show off our sidewalk skills on the luxury of a shiny wooden floor.

PART FOUR

THE GREAT OUTDOORS

FISHING

FISHING IS PROBABLY THE FIRST ATTEMPT MOST kids make at conquering the wild beast. It was a safe enough outdoor sporting activity to be approved by my parents as early as I can remember, yet exciting enough to offer both mystery, and the thrill of the hunt.

Hedgesville afforded us many different fishing venues to try our luck at the sport. We had ponds — Pitzer's and Brown's in town, and McDaniel's and Pingley's a short drive away — several trout streams, and Back Creek, all within walking distance. The Potomac River was several miles away and we went there only with adults.

We always had fishing equipment. My father was an Ocean City level-winder person. If you haven't fished, this probably means nothing to you. The line was camouflaged and the rod was metal. He was an expert at casting and rarely had a backlash. My brother and I began with bait-casting reels that weren't level-winders, and created many bird nests out of our line. Our supply of tackle was kept in a small, semi-rusted metal box, and usually consisted of: loose hooks; sinkers; a jar of rotting salmon eggs; a knife; a stringer; and a few dehydrated worms, some still attached to hooks. Dad was a live-bait purist, while Uncle Charles sometimes dabbled in the artificial variety. He gave me my first spinning reel and fiberglass rod, and a black-and-orange flatfish bait. I still have that bait some 50 years later.

Fishing trips required bait in the form of worms. You didn't buy them; you dug them. Uncle Fred lived down the road about a quarter of a mile. There was a small stream on the back of his property, covered by large willow trees, next to Pitzer's pond. The ground there was always wet and we kept a shovel nearby to dig worms. This part of his property always looked like it had been bombed. He didn't care. All he asked for were some fish, and he got them often. He kept a knife and pan outside his back porch for cleaning.

Catching night crawlers was another way of obtaining our bait. On damp nights we set out after dark with a flashlight and coffee can. There's a real art to catching night crawlers — an activity designed for the young of *back*. Bending over for a long time as a kid is okay, but it hurts as you get older. We stored the worms in a barrel buried in the ground under a big maple tree at the end of our garden.

Pond fishing was just what you would expect — you could catch lots of blue gills and bass. Each pond had its own unique inventory. You always caught fish, and the only problem was deciding which ones to keep. Bass eat the small blue gills and get quite large. They were the top prize and were usually released if caught. Ponds are best fished late in the evening, just before dark, and many times we came home after dark.

These were the days of an actual trout season. We eagerly anticipated it for weeks in advance. Well before sunrise, we grabbed our equipment, jumped on our bikes, and peddled off to a choice location. You could start fishing at daylight. The trout streams were only three or four feet wide, with many hiding spots for the trout. Pulling such large fish out of such a small body of water always surprised me. Trout were good eating and always brought home for dinner.

Some fishermen would bring their catches home and release them in the ponds around town. Brown's pond was a popular destination for these fish transplants and became over-stocked at times. To reduce the population, the Department of Natural Resources would bring in large nets and pull tons of fish from the pond, dump them into large buckets, and place them on trucks to be transplanted in yet another location. As expected, we saw many sunfish. When the nets revealed larger fish, we always ran to see them. Bass weighed three to four pounds, and had always been our goal. What we did not expect to see, and had never caught while fishing there, were the enormous catfish. The most exciting revelation, however, was a huge goldfish weighing more than five pounds! Someone's fish bowl once held this monster in its infancy. As they are in the carp family and are bottom-feeders, they'll grow in proportion to the container in which they are kept. Seeing them in park ponds today is commonplace, but for us that day at Brown's pond, it was a miracle to behold.

Trips to Back Creek could last the whole day. Typically we brought along hot dogs, a loaf of bread, and soda to sustain us. Sometimes we engaged in serious fishing, and other times we just swam and skipped rocks. Back Creek was shallow, we could see the bottom, and we rarely found water that was over our heads.

When taken to the river to fish, things totally changed. The Potomac River was large, wide, and often had a strong current. Slow water meant lazy fishing with poles resting in Y-shaped sticks stuck in the ground. We sat and talked, or even slept. When the water was high and muddy, we caught lots of mud cats or yellow catfish, but we didn't eat them. My brother would sometimes light a firecracker and stick it in the mouth of an unlucky fish, and toss it into the woods. You can imagine what happened.

For trips to the Potomac River and Dam #5, we added bloody chicken livers, rotten shrimp, and dough balls to our inventory of bait. Liver and shrimp were used to catch catfish, and dough balls were used for carp. To our tackle supply we also added a rod with snag hooks. Fishing there meant slow water above the dam, and we caught bass in daytime and eels at night. Below the dam was very fast water — especially in the race — and in the speeding water we snagged carp and caught catfish.

Anyone who has ever fished has fish stories a plenty. We had our own share of fish adventures. Sometimes my Uncle Charles took us on fishing trips to the Shenandoah

River above Harpers Ferry. You would have to see this place to appreciate it. There are exposed rocks and ledges all over the river. We jumped from one rock formation to another, fishing in the deep hole between them in the fast water. One time, I was wearing a heavy coat with pockets full of sodas, and was carrying my fishing equipment. My uncle had jumped ahead to a rock, and was reaching out to grab my hand as I made the leap of several feet. I missed, and fell directly into fast-moving water, well over my head. The current carried me downstream for several yards until I found myself in waist-deep water, and was able to stand up and climb onto some rocks. Just an average day.

Fishing was tremendous fun and nobody ever got hurt — except for one of our dogs who got a fish hook stuck in his foot, which had to be cut out by the vet. We cleaned our catch on the railroad ties by the chicken house. Once we even found a live turtle inside a bass. Mom would perform a final cleaning and inspection before she cooked the fish for supper. Most people today practice catch-and-release. Some only see the world of fish by looking at a box of Mrs. Paul's. Our fish had character. They croaked, wiggled, and fought for their lives. They provided us not only with protein, but also with many hours of fun.

———⚬⚬⚬———

SNAGGING CARP

THE JOKE GOES, "DO YOU KNOW HOW TO COOK a carp? You put it on a pine board, cover it with onions, and cook it for several hours. Then you remove it from the oven, throw away the carp, and eat the board." Carp are large bottom-feeders. They can reach more than 30 pounds in the river and are caught with a meal mixture called dough balls. Carp tasted terrible, but we caught them because they were impressively large and put up a good fight.

We had a better, semi-illegal way of catching carp for sport, and it was called "snagging." This required a super heavy-duty steel rod, a reel, a 50–60 pound test camouflage line, and a leather glove. Onto the line you would tie two or three treble hooks and heavy lead weights.

With equipment in hand, we went to the Potomac River and Dam #5. Walking past the dam and toward the power house you could hear the sound of high speed turbines. The entire flow of the river was reduced to a width of 50 feet as water channeled under the power house, it turned the turbines. It was at the corner of this structure — where the water exited the turbines — that we wanted to be.

Our location for snagging carp was probably near the

top of the list of the most dangerous places you could go around Hedgesville. I don't think my mother realized how dangerous it was, because if she did, she wouldn't have let my Uncle Charles take us there. To reach it you slid down a 30-foot bank of cinders and gravel. At the bottom were several railroad ties anchored into the bank. This provided a ledge about 12 inches wide on which to stand. In front of you the water churned and boiled up as it left the turbines. Downstream from where we stood, the bank consisted of basketball-sized stones. On the other side was a tall concrete wall running the entire length of the race. Both sides eventually sloped down to level ground some 50 yards downstream. The water flowed at a very fast rate in this confined area. One slip and you were gone, pulled under by the suction and eventually spit out somewhere downstream.

In this spot would collect all the fish heading upstream. We didn't have to catch them with bait, but rather just snag them with one of our large hooks. You would drop about eight feet of line into the water near the corner of the building. While standing on the narrow ledge, you would just jerk up the pole, hoping to snag a fish.

Sometimes you got nothing for several minutes, and sometimes you could feel the hooks brush against a fish, but only find a scale attached. If you repeated this enough times, you would eventually snag a fish. You could hook them in any part of their body. In the black swirling water, you never knew what was on the end of your line.

Most fish would end up downstream. Their swimming force, combined with the speed of the water in the race, would cause the reel to whine as line was let out. You'd try with little success to control the drag by pressing your thumb against the line still spooled on the reel. Mostly you'd walk downstream along wet rocks, following the fish.

At the end of the race, the water spread out to join the river again. Here you stood your ground. You could begin reeling the fish in a little at a time, and if you were lucky, you'd finally see a fish on the end of you line, being pulled toward the shore. Finally, you could grab it and, with prize in hand, make your way back up towards the power house. It could be any size from 2 to 30 pounds. We'd pass a rope through its gills and anchor the fish to the ledge. Why we kept them, I don't really know. Sometimes we took them to the local tavern or stopped to give them to someone.

This was snagging carp. It was our version of sport fishing. Each catch was a new adventure with stories that could be retold as we prepared for our next trip.

———

THE LEAKY SIEVE

THIS WAS THE NAME GIVEN TO A GREEN-COLORED wooden boat my uncle and his friends used. It was our only boat for the river and creek. It wasn't equipped with motor or oars, but was propelled by a long pole.

In winter we would sink it, and chain it to a tree. This was necessary to keep the wood swollen so as not to leak. It only partially worked. In the spring we would pull the 14-foot, submerged object close enough to shore to start bailing it out. Little by little, more boat than water would appear.

Eventually it would float. Still holding several inches of water, it required what seemed like constant bailing using a large coffee can. In Back Creek, this didn't much matter, but on the river, it was much more serious. The creek was shallow and calm; not the case for the Potomac River.

Once, while using the boat in the river below the dam, the pole broke. There was nothing to do but ride it out. Fortunately there are small islands, one of which we hit. The water was too swift to swim or pull the boat back to the river bank, so we found a limb and used it as pole. We made it back across and pulled the boat back up the river to the dam and continued to fish. Just another fishing trip.

———

BOY ON AN AIR MATTRESS

D AM #5 IS A TALL CONCRETE STRUCTURE ALONG the Potomac River, with countless large rocks below. The water behind the dam is very deep, but doesn't always flow over it. Dam #5 has been the scene of accidents and even death. Back then, there were no markers in the river to indicate a dam ahead. The top of the dam is about 18 inches thick. I have seen people approach the dam, shut off their motor, and slide the front of their boat onto the concrete top. I have performed some fairly risky feats, but this was beyond me.

The craziest thing I ever saw at the dam involved a boy and his dog. During a summer rainstorm, a young boy lay facedown on an air mattress and pushed off from the Maryland side of the river, and headed toward the West Virginia side. Water was flowing just inches over the dam, and the current was extremely swift. This was dangerous enough, but add to it the fact that he had a dog sitting between his legs — unbelievable but true. He made it all the way across without going over the edge or being sucked into the turbines. We just sat there and shook our heads, wondering what that kid was thinking.

—∞—

Hunting

OPPORTUNITIES TO HUNT WERE EVERYWHERE. In the fall, I would come home from school, change clothes, grab my gun, and head out into the woods — a childhood ritual that today, is totally unheard of in our area. Hunting was fun, partly due to the powerful feeling it gave me to possess a weapon. It didn't require much planning. We needed no four-wheelers or fancy attire. We didn't even have to go far to find game, and would stay out until dark.

My mother always had a fear of guns and constantly gave us the same safety warnings. My father owned a .22 rifle and there was a pistol or two in a drawer, but they were off-limits. Uncle Charles was the great hunter in the family. He was the first to allow me to shoot a shotgun. He told me the .12 gauge would kick a little so I braced my shoulder against a tree. When it went off, my shoulder got pushed back into the tree, creating a big sore bruise. He then advised me against doing that. I quickly learned. I acquired a .410 bolt action. It was perfect and more powerful than the .22, but with less kick than the .12 gauge.

If squirrels were our target, we'd head up the hill behind us to the Wood's property. Across the road from my house and through the graveyard was a thicket and wooded area where we found rabbits. Turkeys were harder to find and required more patience, though one was actually shot on the sidewalk beside Poisal's Store. We shot muskrats near the grade school and made box traps and snares to catch rabbits in that same area. We shot pigeons in barns with BB guns. Deer hunting required the use of slugs in the shotgun. There were some deer near home, but they were not as plentiful as they are today. Deer hunting was more of an adult thing, and we didn't do a lot of it as kids.

We had a problem with skunks. They hung around the barn and chicken house and thought the garden was theirs. We taped a flashlight to the barrel of the .22 and would hunt them after dark. You could see them only a few feet from the house. You had to be very careful when shooting them as there were houses around us. Once, we even shot one that was completely white. The risk of being sprayed by a skunk just went along with the territory. My father was once a victim of a good skunk-spraying. I remember him stripping down to his underwear beside the kitchen and taking a colorful bath in pure tomato juice.

The story of owning a gun took an unusual twist after graduating from high school. I took a summer job working for the state road department where I was put with two gentlemen who only did things their way. One of them wanted a shotgun, and so I decided to trade my .410 shotgun with him for a .22 rifle. I went to his house in Martinsburg and test fired his gun by shooting it out the open kitchen door. The trade was complete. A year or so later, I was hunting with my friend Craig. He had a single-shot shotgun that he claimed had a faulty firing pin. He said he would trade it with me for my rifle. I agreed, not even knowing what gun he had. I just figured it would be better than what I had. It ended up being a .16 gauge Beretta. It was a model in which the barrel folded into the stock. It was rather fancy — much fancier than any of the utilitarian weapons that I had ever used. I still have this gun, and it has never caused me any trouble.

My daughter, Stephanie, was an exchange student in Italy in 1989 and spent the summer with the Moretti family, who happened to be relatives of the Beretta Arms Company family. Stephanie, Gula, and I were invited back to Italy in the Summer of 1991. Luigi Moretti — Stephanie's exchange father — gave me a tour of the factory in Val Trumpe, and I got to see how the guns were manufactured. I shared with him the story of how I came to own one. It's a small world.

Guns are viewed in a very different light today. My son, Chuck, never got the chance to experience hunting as I did, although he hunted a little. The area has changed so much over the past few years. Housing developments appear around every turn, and posted signs are found on wooded lands. There is a large public hunting area nearby, but it just isn't the same as walking out your back door carrying a rifle or shotgun, and heading into the woods.

'COON HUNTING

BEFORE THE AGE OF DISCOVERING GIRLS OR MUSIC, there was 'coon hunting. Although stereotyped as a slow talking, Southern backwoods activity today, it was quite the popular after-dark activity for us in the fall.

The object of this sport is simple: finding and killing a raccoon. Items needed to accomplish this were minimal: an eager coondog, a bright flashlight, and a gun. Proper 'coon-hunting attire included boots, along with multiple layers of clothing. You never really knew what the weather would be like, so you wore several shirts, a sweater, and a coat. Not required, but certainly expected, was some form of alcohol.

Training season began in late September. At this time, you could take your dogs out and run 'coons, but not kill them. That was the law, but my Uncle Charles always said it was bad for the dogs not to see the result of their chase. You figure it out.

On one occasion, we were at McCoy's Ferry during training season. We had a gun, of course. As we walked back to the car, we saw lights coming toward us. My uncle said to toss the gun into the woods. Low-and-behold, it was the game warden, and he asked to see our license. I had none, and my uncle said I was only 12 years old and didn't need one. I was older and *did* need one. The warden just stared at all six feet two inches of me. My uncle, seeing the potential problem, said, "If you think he's big, you should see his father. He's a *really* big son-of-a-bitch." It obviously worked and we went on our way. We returned the next day for the gun. A farmer had reported us, suspecting we had been spotlighting deer. We never did that.

Uncle Charles was the undisputed king of 'coon hunting in our family. He always had at least one good dog. Every few years he would order a new one from somewhere down South. It usually arrived sick, but Uncle Charles would nurse it back to health, and it was soon ready to hunt. The names of these dogs included Rinkles, Drum, and Blue. Bluetick coonhounds were always expected to be good hunting dogs. The only true coonhound I owned was a bluetick mixed with some other variety of dog. Performance, not pedigree, was key.

Hunting always began after dark and could last for several hours or all night. Uncle Charles and I would load the dogs into his car and set off. You could hunt almost anywhere. Today these places are gone. You simply opened the car door and out jumped the dogs. They automatically knew what to do. We would gather the light and gun and follow them. Our gun was a single-shot .22. Our flashlight was large and heavy. My uncle worked on the railroad, so our light was a railroad light. It had a bulb as big as a car headlight, and was attached to a very large battery.

We would begin walking, waiting for the sound of barking dogs as they picked up a trail. Interpreting their bark was an art. You had to determine distance, direction, and how hot or cold the trail was. We'd listen, then walk, and keep repeating this until we were sure the trail was fresh. The raccoon will get scared and head for its favorite large tree to scurry up and hide. Many times it will head for its den tree. If the raccoon gets there, you lose.

Once the raccoon is up a tree, the dogs will begin to "bark tree." It's a regular, relentless yelping. Now you have your prey and must go to the dogs because they won't leave the tree. After finding the dogs, we would stir them up by yelling, "Where is he, boy?" and cautiously pat them on the head. Touch was kept to a minimum, as the dogs would be in a carnivorous frenzy. We'd turn on the light to try and find the raccoon. Its eyes would give it away, reflecting light right back at you. You might even discover more than one.

If the tree was climbable and the adults were still sober, someone would climb the tree and shake the raccoon out. More often we would just shoot it. After the raccoon hit the ground, you waited a few seconds while the dogs tossed their trophy around before rushing in and pulling it out, sometimes with dogs still attached. You'd then walk away, trying to get the dogs to move on to another trail. This was repeated until the humans got tired and wanted to go home. Not so for the dogs. They would do it all night.

On some rather uneventful nights we would walk and just stop, sit on logs, and talk. My mother's cousin Doug sometimes hunted with us. My brother and I thought he was the luckiest man in the world. Doug would stretch and loudly proclaim, "Son-of-a-gun — look what I found!"

From under the leaves always appeared a bottle of whiskey. "Somebody must have left it here," he would say. He did this at least once a year. As we got older, we realized that he was that "somebody," but for a while he had us fooled.

There were several ways for a hunt to end. After killing a raccoon, the dogs could be chained and led back to the car, which was not easy. The dogs also had a habit of checking back at the car, and we would sometimes go there and wait for them. Other times we'd yell and yell, trying to get them to come back to us. It occasionally worked, but not always.

If we were close to home and the dogs refused to come with us, we just left them and they would find their way back. If far away from home, we had to stay and wait for them. They might return to the car as a pack, but usually appeared one at a time, at their leisure. We let the car idle to keep warm while we waited. As the dogs appeared, we'd get out and toss them in. They smelled bad, but sharing the warm car with them was more appealing than waiting in the cold. If the pack took too long to arrive, the car would run out of gas, and we resigned ourselves to just waiting there until daylight. On one occasion I was awakened by a flashlight pushed against the window. My father was leading the search party and he got the vehicle running.

Most often we came home after only a couple of hours. We skinned the raccoons, nailed their hides to my uncle's garage, and he later sold them. You can eat raccoon. I have done it and as I like to joke, "It tastes just like raccoon."

There are so many stories about 'coon hunting that it's tempting not to write more. We looked forward to each hunt, but today I wonder why. Usually we were too hot or too cold, and logged many miles each night. Sometimes our dogs would cross a creek, and we had to follow. Hunting in the nearby public hunting area — Sleepy Creek — was a wild and isolating experience in the 1950s. Bobcats were common, and hearing one of them made the hair on the back of your neck stand up. Sometimes we'd cry back at them and their sounds would grow closer. We kids would get scared. Walking through the dark woods with a heavily bleeding raccoon tossed over your shoulder and tree limbs smacking you in the face doesn't have much appeal today.

My wife and I drive down local roads today and I tell her that I used to go 'coon hunting here or there. Homes are almost everywhere now, leaving only small patches of woods. Sleepy Creek still exists, and you can walk for miles, but the sport isn't too popular. I guess we are just too busy today to sit and listen to dogs bark.

—∞∞∞—

NEIGHBORHOOD YOUTH CORPS

T HE SUMMER OF 1964 GOT ME OUT OF THE close confines of home and into the workforce with strangers and many new adventures. At the age of 16, I went looking for a summer job that would pay some good bucks. There were none in town, so I went to the unemployment office in Martinsburg.

I wasn't alone in my search, as several other boys I knew were also there looking for work. At first we were told that no jobs were available, but they later said there was a new Neighborhood Youth Corps (NYC) program. In order to get one of the jobs, your parents had to be at, or below, the poverty level. Our parents had jobs, and although we had little money, we didn't qualify. Returning home, it seemed I would be back in the orchards. Several days later I got a call. Not enough qualified applicants had applied for the NYC positions, and I could have one if I still wanted it.

The NYC jobs were at Sleepy Creek Public Hunting and Fishing Area. Today, people new to the area see Sleepy Creek as an island of wilderness in a sea of development. I see it as it was in 1964 and before. It was wild. I knew the place rather well from previous hunting and camping trips.

It consisted of 23,000 acres of wilderness, with a few roads, and a large, man-made lake. It had been purchased from the White Oak Lumber Company, which had harvested much of the timber. The state bought it to be kept as a forest, but later converted it into a hunting and fishing area. Sleepy Creek was managed by George Lewis, who looked, walked, and dressed like a drill instructor. He only knew how to do things one way — his way. Things had only one place to belong and one condition to be placed therein. He lived at Sleepy Creek with his wife and children. His children were slightly younger than I was.

The 1964 NYC gang consisted of about a dozen of us kids — half from Martinsburg and the rest from the Hedgesville area. I was in my element, but the Martinsburg kids were like fish out of water. They didn't even know how to dress for working in the woods. The differences between us made for some interesting situations. We boys from Hedgesville met at the grocery in Tomahawk, and piled into one car to make the trek to work. My parents allowed me to take my turn driving the family 1959 Chevy station wagon. Other kids did the same. The Martinsburg boys arrived in similar ways, but seemed to have a more sporadic attendance pattern than we did.

Sleepy Creek was wild, bug and snake infested, and dusty with Morgan County red shale. We were not allowed to use power tools, so everything we did was done by hand. We each were given a brush ax that we marked as our own for the summer. George instructed us on how to sharpen it, both by file, and with a grindstone attached to a washing machine motor. Our jobs were not sophisticated. We cut brush to create places for deer to browse. We cleared more brush along the dirt roads and fields, dumped trash, filled in holes in the road, and cut more brush. It was hard, hot, dirty work. Within 30 minutes, you were soaked to the skin with sweat.

There was no fooling around with George. The few times he laughed were not because something was funny, but because someone, according to him, had made a mistake. This only seemed to affirm his perfection. He expected you to do your work and do it correctly. He had a swagger when he walked, being very stiff above the waist, and usually had a pipe in his mouth.

George had a specific way of doing everything. Trees were cut first in the center of the selected area, and you moved outward from that spot so as to be in the shade as long as possible. Rocks and dirt were moved and placed in precise locations. Digging shale from the pit followed an exact pattern. Tools had to be cleaned and stored according to his exacting standards. Outlines of each hand tool were painted on the walls, so there was no excuse for not placing them back where they belonged. Oil cans had to be placed on metal racks in order to collect every drop of residual oil for future use. Even his lunch was perfectly structured. He ate saltine crackers with peanut butter in between, which were wrapped in waxed paper. The paper was saved and used again and again. He washed down his lunch with a thermos of hot coffee. It was always the same.

We, on the other hand, were a rag-tag lot of boys, and were dressed in every conceivable form and combination of clothing. Lunch mostly meant the ability to actually sit down under a shade tree. Our meals ranged from nothing at all to a bag of junk food. We had no refrigeration, so you had to be careful what you brought. George enjoyed making fun of at least one item someone had brought. We carried a can filled with water that we usually got at one of the springs on the property. As the summer progressed, we talked George into letting us bring some ice from home to put in the water. We eventually got him to allow us to put some sugar-baby watermelons in the water can to eat at lunch.

Sleepy Creek was full of rattlesnakes, and we killed countless numbers of them over the summer. Their skins were coated with a tanning paste of borax and sulphur before being nailed to boards to dry. Once, a worker got mad at another kid from Martinsburg, and when George wasn't around, made him tilt back large rocks and look for snakes. He found one and quickly dropped the rock. He was forced to lift it up again, and the snake — quite mad by now — was killed. The boy got so angry that he stormed off, saying he was quitting and would walk home. Home was many miles and hours away on foot. He never made it but went just far enough away to be out of the group's sight. We picked him up that evening, took him home, and never saw him again. Several others quit before the summer was over.

We couldn't wait for pay day, which never seemed to arrive. We were paid twice a month, but the first two weeks were held back, so it was a month before any money was seen. Some of the guys had borrowed money against their future pay, and when it finally arrived, they were just about broke. The idea was to have us save some money for use during the school year. A day or two after being paid, it was obvious this wasn't going to happen. Some boys showed up with a lot of new items, most of which had a short life expectancy. I, on the other hand, was always very frugal, and thought long and hard before spending anything.

Over the summer, George told us many tales, and shared his knowledge of history, nature, and folklore. He told us about the possible burial of gold by British General Edward Braddock during the French and Indian War in 1755. He shared the story of John Myers and the white deer. The Myers family had been the central family in that area. He showed us the remains of their homestead as well as a very unusual ceremonial-type formation of rock benches and an altar on top of some cliffs. George knew most trees and animals and was eager to share this information. Some kids from Martinsburg had never seen such things. He got a kick out of having them eat plants that were less than tasty and stung their mouths. Once, a few minutes after they ate the plants, he told them not to worry as the antidote was to drink some milk. Where were they going to get milk?

I enjoyed my summer jobs at Sleepy Creek. Having the opportunity to work on so much of the land allowed me to gain a unique familiarity with the place. It's neat that I can remember walking the stream bed before it became a lake, and that as a member of my school band, I performed there for that lake's dedication.

A dozen or so years later, I ran into George at the grocery store. I told him I was teaching school, and he asked if I wanted a summer job back at Sleepy Creek. I agreed, and took a job as supervisor of the Governor's Summer Youth Program for kids in trouble or at risk, many coming from a residential group home. It was ironic, and enjoyable, to be working again with George, and I was able to learn a lot more from him. I worked that job for several summers, well past George's retirement. I even helped to break-in his replacement.

My summer jobs in the Neighborhood Youth Corps at Sleepy Creek marked both the end of my childhood years, and of hanging around Hedgesville. I learned to work hard and appreciate my pay. It expanded my thinking, and taught me a lot about the world of plants and animals, which later aided in my teaching of biology. I still have many of the snake skins and animal skulls I collected at Sleepy Creek.

After the summer of 1964, there was no going back. Although Hedgesville would always be "home," my world was getting larger. My future lay ahead of me like a newly opened book, and I was eager to discover all of the new experiences in store for me just ahead. I don't think this is really so unusual. I guess I was just growing up.

AFTERWORD

AFTER READING THIS BOOK YOU MAY BE CURIOUS why I chose the summer of 1964 as its stopping point. The reason is simple: I turned 16, got my driver's license, and could travel as far as my car and wallet would take me. I could now work, study, play music, and meet new people beyond the town limits of Hedgesville. With this freedom and the privilege of mobility came new responsibilities. My parents' expectations for me grew, and they began treating me less like a kid and more like an adult. Turning 16 was so much more than just getting one year older. It opened up adulthood, and life's endless possibilities.

This book marks the end of my childhood stories, but not the end of my writing. As the first printing of this book was released, I began writing about my adventures beyond 1964. Now, as the second printing of this book takes place, "Book Two" is written and awaiting editing. I look forward to sharing this next chapter of my life with you.

Visit www.girlsonpress.com to see upcoming author events; to sign up for book release updates; to write a personal book review; or to inquire about scheduling an author appearance, reading, or book signing at your next event or book club gathering.

ACKNOWLEDGEMENTS

THANKS TO MY FAMILY, FRIENDS, AND THE PEOPLE of Hedgesville who made my childhood wonderful, and worth remembering and sharing. Without you there would be no *Stories from a Small Town*.

Thanks to my wife, Gula, for your amazing creativity, your constant encouragement, and for your wonderful way with words. Your finishing touches made all the difference.

Many thanks to Irene, Janice, Jenny, Kay, Liz, and Scott, for generously offering to read the book at various stages of completion, and for your collective proofreading efforts.

Special thanks to my son, Chuck, for offering a fresh set of eyes when we really, really needed it.

Thank you to Jimmy, for continuing to answer the phone when I called, and for sharing your local knowledge.

Thank you to Peggy, for letting my grandson, Edward, be spontaneously photographed on your porch one day.

Finally, deepest thanks to my editor-in-chief, designer, and publisher — my daughter, Stephanie — for taking on this project. Without your diverse skills, steady guidance, and determination, this book would have continued to be just a stack of handwritten pages in a file cabinet. I'm glad your mother and I sent you to art school.

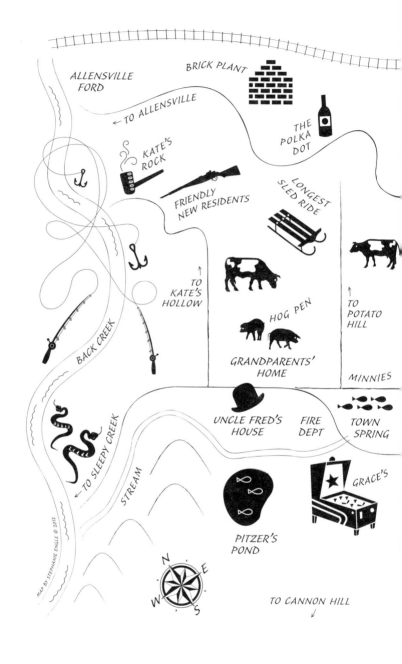

ABOUT THE AUTHOR

Roger Engle spent the first 21 years of his life in the small town of Hedgesville, West Virginia, surrounded by his grandparents, parents, siblings, and a large, extended family. He graduated from Hedgesville High School and went on to receive a Bachelor of Science degree from Shepherd College (now Shepherd University) in nearby Shepherdstown, West Virginia. Mr. Engle taught biology at South Hagerstown High School in Hagerstown, Maryland, for 30 years. While teaching there he completed graduate studies and received an advanced professional certificate from the State of Maryland. He also served in the United States Army Reserve.

Mr. Engle has been married to his wife, Gula, for 44 years and they have two children, six grandchildren, and an ever-increasing number of great-grandchildren. After retiring from teaching, he has become very active in his hometown community of Martinsburg, West Virginia, volunteering, and serving on various boards and committees.

Mr. Engle spends his leisure time enjoying his family, gardening, traveling, eating lots of barbecue as a certified judge of the Kansas City Barbeque Society, and, of course, writing.